The Junk Truck
A Gritty Junk Haul Tell-All

By: Travis Geier

ISBN (Print): 978-1-7377050-0-0
ISBN (eBook): 978-1-7377050-1-7
Edited by: Emma Lenar
Cover art by: Waterpop.art
Author photo by: Brandonevans.art
Thejunktruck.com

This book is dedicated to anyone who lives in the shadows because of their mental illness, learning disabilities, or addiction.

Table of Contents

The Junk Truck

Prologue

At the age of 29, after posting a bicycle for sale, I was made fun of online for my grammar. It hurt so bad when the evil comments about my writing showed up in my feed. It stung so much that I went to the Waukesha County Technical College to assess my grammar skills. I was told that I had the writing level of a second-grader. I was toying with the idea of going back to school to work on my grammar and composition skills. I even called Sylvan Learning Center to see if they would teach me; turns out they strictly teach kids.

After a few months of studying on my own, I received an envelope in the mail for English classes at the Waukesha County Technical College. I took this as a sign, so I went back to school to learn grammar. I was determined to be competent in writing. The school wanted me to study to get an associate's degree in something practical, but I had other plans.

Being a big Garfield fan my whole life, I always loved reading, so my goal was to write my own book! Over the years of studying, I faced addiction and mental illness, but I always pushed forward to write my own book. Eventually, I had gained the writing level of an early college student. I felt confident that I could write the book now. They say to start out writing about what you know best, so I wrote this book about the one part of my life that I felt defined me.

1

The biggest part of my life that defined me to my peers was that I ran a junk removal business called The Junk Truck. I was known as the junk man around my community. I started the business because I suffer from type one bipolar disorder, so The Junk Truck was a means to support myself. Eventually, mental illness got the best of me. The business had a sad ending, but my association with the company was something that I couldn't shake. I tried to redefine myself as a comedian, writer, and a Youtuber, but in the end, I would always be associated as a junk man.

I would always get asked, "How's The Junk Truck going?" I would want to run far away from civilization in these moments. I tried to just forget about the business, but life has an odd way of reminding you of your biggest creations and failures. I went through a long period of feeling ashamed for losing my business to mental illness and addiction. This made me want to tell my story about the triumphs and tragedies of living with mental illness. I maintained a blog at travisvulture.com about my struggles with bipolar disorder but wanted to have something that I could turn into my first book.

When I was 32, I was just getting back on my feet after a manic episode. I was working at a few different junk removal companies. I was just treated like a set of arms that brought up the junk from the cellar for the franchises I worked for. I felt like I didn't have anything that I could call my own anymore. It was after I started working at College Hunks Milwaukee, that I realized how special my junk removal journey had been. I observed all this chaos as a junk man, so I thought that a gritty tale about junk removal might be in the cards.

It was out of frustration that I finally broke down and started to write about my story as a young man that owned a junk removal company and lost it all to mental illness. I was going to use The Junk Truck as the vehicle to tell the gritty tale of being a junk man, but that is interwoven with a story about addiction and mental illness.

This story was very hard to write about, but I hope someone out there reads this and can relate to some of the themes in the book. If you are struggling with mental illness or addiction, please consider talking to someone. Scream, jump, and shout until someone helps you. I think in society we tend to forget the mentally ill, and we force them to live in the shadows. Make sure you are not forgotten about in society. Make yourself known and seek out the right organizations that can give you a helping hand.

This book is a collection of essays about junk removal that is written by a junk man. The essays showcase the dirty jobs of The Junk Truck while following a more linear story of the chaos of my personal life. I have inserted real reviews from our past customers into the beginning of some chapters. Names have been changed to protect the innocent, but all these tales are true. I hope this book entertains you! Enjoy!

The Chase

Red and blue sirens were burning my eyes in my rearview mirror. "I am a mile away from home! I can make it!" What the fuck was making it anyway? "Fuck the police." I had spent most of my life running from those red and blue flashing lights. This time seemed different as my car obeyed every speed limit and made every correct turn signal. I kept collecting new cop cars as I kept driving. With every turn, a new squad would join the pursuit. My mind kept running through what I was going to do, "My plan is to run upstairs after I shove the car in park!" I did a sharp right turn into my parking spot at my parents' house! Slammed the shifter into park! "Here I fucking go, wish me luck!" Let me reverse a little bit and tell you a bit about myself.

I have always made big life mistakes since I can remember. As a child, I barely remember ever doing homework. I just didn't give a fuck; even in elementary school. I got a D in spelling in 4th grade. I caused problems in school, at home, and at my dad's house. I will never understand how at the age of 29, I had the writing skills of a first-quarter second grader. Oh, wait, yes I do; it's because I am a fuck up. I admit that I was a horrible, evil child with undiagnosed bipolar disorder, but somewhere along the way a lot of people gave up on me.

School, authority, and working have never been in the blood of the Geiers. My grandpa was

4

once wanted by the F.B.I. because of something he allegedly did while he was involved in a biker gang. My grandpa and his family had to go into hiding because the F.B.I. was looking for my grandpa. They hid out under different aliases for close to a decade. When my grandpa turned himself in, they moved back to Wisconsin to start over. My grandpa got off, but his biker mentality was always present in my upbringing. My grandpa started glorifying the violent acts that he did with the gang when I was just five years old. I remember being five and my mom pleading with my grandpa to not tell me old gang stories. She said, "Please, Dad! Fucking don't." My grandpa promised to not tell me any. The second my mom's car left the driveway, he raced me down to this mobile home he converted into a bike shop. It was there that he showed me the Swastika, gang colors, and told me stories of gang violence. I believe that this type of exposure to the underworld led me down a path of destruction in my childhood.

In my high school years, it came time at Oconomowoc High School for my guidance counselor meeting to decide my future. My mom took off of work to attend the appointment. My guidance counselor sat us down in a very cozy suburban school office and politely asked, "Travis, what do you want to do with the rest of your life?"

Without a blink, I blurted out, "I am going to be a homeless bum!" Next, in my mania, I spat, "I am going to just live on the streets!"

My guidance counselor politely questioned my authority by asking, "How will you make money then?"

I jumped out of my chair and said, "I will beg on the streets for it!" Even with my mother's tan skin, she was flushed with pumping, red embarrassment.

The room became stale and awkward in the air. The counselor eventually gave up and showed us to the door. Years later, my mom still brings up that meeting with a half laugh and a touch of sadness.

The plan was to drop out of Oconomowoc High School because I was a senior with the credits of a first-quarter freshman. My friend's mom taught troubled teens like me, and she insisted that I drop out to get my H.S.E.D.. On my 18th birthday, December 20th, 2006, I dropped out of high school.

When I dropped out, I did the exact opposite of what my friend's mom said to do. Instead of getting my H.S.E.D., I did the next best thing, which was to become a total burnout. I slept on blankets at my mom's house in my disgusting room, filled with chicken bones, bloody tampons, and a couch flipped over sideways that draped blankets for an 18-year-old boy's fort. I was a total mentally ill slob who hoarded nasty chicken bones and my girlfriend's soiled feminine products. I was a seriously sick fuck. I would get so fucking stoned every day and sleep. I worked part-time at a Pick N Save as a grocery bagger.

That summer, my mom moved to a house on a channel on Lower Nemahbin Lake in Summit. My stepdad thought I was a scummy, bipolar freak, so he was angry to find out that my mom was to bring her dirtball son with her to their lake paradise.

It was around this time that I started to attend the Waukesha County Technical College for my H.S.E.D.. I became very determined to get my diploma. That is when I made a life-changing mistake that would lead me to my wild experiences in the scrapping and junk removal worlds.

Now, let's return to our regularly scheduled program! We return to how I fucked up my entire life for the next few years already in progress.

I was in love with the porno grind band Anal Blast. The band was led by Don Decker who also was severely mentally ill like me. Anal Blast had a lot of songs about menstrual blood and also had disgusting merchandise. I had met Don Decker, lead vocalist, outside a show at Station 4 in Minneapolis once, but now they were coming to Milwaukee for a metal fest at the Rave. There was no fucking way I was going to miss such hits as: "Bloody Mary's Bloody Cunt" or "Menstrual Pancakes."

I woke up that morning, smoked a bowl in my room, and went to Brownberry Bread to submit an application for employment.

I wanted to appease my stepdad because he had hired me to paint the garage at the new lake house, but the project took me most of the summer. Honestly, the reason being that I smoked my brains out all summer and would fall asleep in the afternoons. Fuck, I would even toke up on the ladder while doing my brush strokes. For this reason, I drove across town to put my application in at the bread factory.

On the way back, the police turned on their lights for me. The problem was that I didn't have my license so I decided not to stop for the police, leading them on a low-speed chase. Hell, I even used my blinker to turn at a stoplight. I had one mile to go before home, sweet home. I looked in my rearview mirror and saw over 10 squad cars. I pulled onto Elm Street and squealed into my little dirt spot in the driveway. I shoved my car in Park and ran into my mother's house. My mom came out screaming as the police were shouting, "Stop and resist!" I quickly jolted upstairs and closed my mom's office and locked it. Suddenly, a foot came through the cheap, white door.

One kick was all it took and I was staring down the barrel of a cop's gun. They shoved my face in the white carpet I had excessively orgasmed all over while watching porn on my mom's computer. My face was deep in the orange crust of my old cum that stained the white carpet. I was being handcuffed as they told me I had just committed a felony by fleeing from law enforcement. They asked me why I ran.

"Because I didn't want my car towed." The pigs were astonished, started laughing, and informed me they would have let me go.

I spent the weekend in Waukesha County Jail. After my release, I had to live with my grandpa. He made me fill out over 30 job applications, but no one would hire me. My grandpa reached out to an acquaintance who owned a thrift store. The guy reluctantly hired me. It was here that I started to daydream about what my next step would actually be.

All my life, I had set what I thought to be unrealistic career goals. As a kid, I wanted to be a cartoonist like Jim Davis, the creator of Garfield. In middle school, I wanted to be a WWE wrestler like Mankind, Cactus Jack, and Dude Love. In my teenage years, I wanted to be a death metal vocalist like Chris Barnes of Cannibal Corpse/Six Feet Under fame. Upon dropping out, I wanted to be a marijuana grower like Jorge Cervantes. I kept setting these goals that, in Wisconsin, would be harder to achieve. I really wanted a career that had nothing to do with corporate America. I wanted a job that went against "the man."

Working at the thrift store was the first time I saw someone scrap metal. It was a hot Summer Wisconsin day. A rusty, white truck with a humongous bed with old wood sides rattled up. Out popped an elderly Spanish gentleman and his sidekick. His partner was a greasy, trucker-looking guy. He had a black mesh trucker hat on, a cut-off Miller High Life shirt, and raggedy cut-off jeans. The drifter sparked up a cigarette and started to load the scrap metal the thrift store had accumulated. The Spanish gentleman lived in Waukesha; he would pick up his workers from the Salvation Army Homeless Shelter. It was in that moment, with this greasy guy glistening in the sun, that I had found my way to be a bum! I asked the two why they hauled it off. They gave a bullshit response that made me realize to ask someone else.

It just happened that a friend's dad I worked with at a Sentry Grocery Store was doing his community service at the thrift store for pulling a gun on someone. I made friends with my buddy's dad and he explained how hot the scrap metal market was at that time in 2007. The shooter explained how to turn the metal in, where, and some prices. My buddy's dad gave me the initial idea to take a few aluminum pots and pans home at a time, so I did, and over the course of a few months, I stored scrap at my stepdad's lake house. When I told my parents about the idea of scrapping metal, they refused the idea. I would not relent on turning the side yard into a scrap business. I think they ended up seeing how much I took an interest in scrapping, so they gave me the green light as long as I placed a brown tarp over the pile.

The pile of aluminum and stainless steel pots grew gigantic. It was beginning to look like an eyesore so I made arrangements with my grandpa, who was my manager at the thrift store, to use his van to test my theory about recycling metal as my job. Meanwhile, my stepdad bought a self-published book, written by a scrapper, on the dos and don'ts of hauling metal for a living.

The grandpa that showed me swastikas and was wanted by the F.B.I. was my manager at the thrift store. He allowed me to cherry-pick all the non-ferrous metal away from the old Spanish guy. It did come at a cost though. For some reason, he was jealous of me, so he forced me to rent the van for hundreds of dollars off the top of my scrap payout on my money. My dear old granddad knew I didn't have a way to get the cookware to Waukesha for my payday without his van.

Now let's talk about the van: it was a beat-up white van from the Navy. It had white metal cages on the windows that looked like you were hauling inmates. The gas pedal on the jenky paddywagon would stop accelerating at certain points. My grandpa had also stuffed the van with a Halloween skeleton corpse and I would see him out and about driving with a corpse as his passenger. It was going to be a deathtrap to drive my pile in with this pile.

I was so fucking angry at my grandpa for abusing his power in that way to take advantage of me like that. I mean fuck, I was willing to put gas back in, but a few hundred bucks off the top? I ended up agreeing because I let everyone walk all over me until I have the mindset of a mass shooter.

I will admit that I was very scared to go into a scrap metal yard because of the "My dong is bigger than yours" complex men have. All my life my dad called me a pansy, so I never felt like a man growing up. Because of this reason, I took a few test drives to Miller Compressing in Waukesha before my big van heist with the loot. I spent that weekend bashing off the plastic handles on the pot and pans to make them what they told me was cleaner metal and worth more money. I "rented the van," loaded up the cookware, and took off for Miller Compressing in Waukesha.

I was so fucking scared to pull in but did anyway. I got out and a short hippie came out of the warehouse in a hard hat with safety glasses on. This person was Shane Love. He was a scrap hippie who traveled to these hippie communes in the woods known as Rainbow Gatherings. I was shaking when he approached and I trembled out, "I don't know what any of these metals are."

He looked at me and said, "Keep calm man; I will help you out!" We spent the next twenty minutes or so separating scrap. He showed me what the difference was and how to test forms of ferrous and non-ferrous metals with a magnet; meanwhile, I told him that I would hook him up with some really dank weed. Shane Love was originally from Oregon. His grandfather scrapped all his life, so scrapping was in his blood. I ended up exchanging numbers with him and he handed me a receipt for my scrap. I purposely didn't look at the amount because I wanted to be surprised. I scanned my ticket at the ATM and 450 dollars fell out of the outdated machine. I was fucking stunned! I had never made that kind of money in one day! I knew right then and there that this was the anti-society way to make your living. I had figured out how to be the bum!

Sierra

At two hundred a pop in royalty fees to "rent the van" from my grandpa, I was going to need my own set of wheels to haul scrap. My uncle Dave was a mechanic of sorts, and we would go look at trucks off Craigslist on the weekends. I had saved exactly three thousand dollars by working at the Catholic thrift store, so finding a good truck in my price range was going to be tricky. We looked at a truck that had a rusted bed that wouldn't be able to sustain the weight of the loads of metal. We looked at another that didn't run. It seemed I may not find a decent truck to drive off the lot in, so to speak. My uncle Dave suggested that we go to the Elkhorn, Wisconsin swap meet.

It was a beautiful sunny day to drive out to Elkhorn. The sky was blue and the grass was green. My uncle being a mechanic, he wanted to get there right at the start of the event to find Mustang parts.

We walked through the aisles of car parts, tools, and automobile collectibles. Still, no sign of a scrap truck. We had these homemade mint chocolate bars with sunflower seeds out of a food truck. The chocolate melted in the hot sun as I orgasmed over the gooey mint dripping with chocolate.

My uncle kept saying that more people might show up to sell their trucks and to not lose hope. At the last hour of being there, my uncle said, "Let's take one more look through all the rows." We started to gaze through all the aisles of car crap. That is when we saw the beast.

Parked in the corner with an old long wooden trailer attached, was a very dark green, 1986 GMC Sierra. The truck had a stake bed put on it with warped wood fencing sides.

The bed of the truck and trailer were full of tools for sale. The front window had a for sale sign in the front window. My uncle and I looked at each other with a grin and said, "Let's go check it out."

A thin, old man with a hat came out of the shadows of the GMC Sierra parked in the corner by the trees. He spoke with a very soft tone as he popped the hood and let us see the underbelly of the beast. My uncle looked over the motor while the guy fired the pig up in one start.

I could tell Dave thought this was a good truck, and the guy wanted exactly $3,000 for the truck and the trailer; that was the exact number that reflected my bank statement. Dave pulled me aside and told me to offer the gentlemen 100 dollars for a hold on the truck until I could wipe out my account in full.

The soft-spoken gentlemen accepted my offer for the hold and gave me his number. He said he needed the truck to haul the tools that didn't sell back to his home in Salem, Wisconsin. I called later that week and we arranged to meet at his house. We drove out to the farm town of Salem which is on the border of Wisconsin and Illinois. I didn't know how to drive with a trailer so my mother drove the truck and trailer out to our home in Oconomowoc. We pulled in and took photos of me posing with my new scrap machine.

Over the next few weekends, we repainted the truck a new green and built new wooden sides. I test drove the truck a lot in a Kmart parking lot and the Olympia Resort hotel to get a feel for truck driving.

By this time, I was ready to start scrapping, so I posted ads on Craigslist for free metal pickup. I used the name Lake Country Scrap Removal and had professional logos made by my stepdad. He was a really good graphic designer that has worked in advertising all his life. I printed my own business cards and we were off to the races to catch Sparky.

Lake Country Scrap Removal

In 2008, sheet iron was 350 bucks a ton. Non-ferrous scrap was at its height of value, too. China was buying all our dirty scrap for their industrialization. At first, I was making very good money by hauling scrap for free out of people's homes.

That summer was very profitable for me, but as the leaves fell to signify autumn, the sale of sheet iron also fell from 350 a ton to 30 bucks a ton. There was no longer any money to profit off of scrap because of the drop in the scrap market. What was I going to do?

I started to pile up an ungodly amount of metal in the side yard where my truck slept. I had a neighbor who looked like Colonel Sanders named Jerry. He had a wife named Margo that was full of zest for her age. They were the most understanding neighbors to have when you are running an illegal scrapyard out of your parents' home.

Jerry had a beautiful yard with colorful flowers, fresh lawn cut, and beautiful outdoor art and trinkets. Next to Jerry's lake paradise was a scrap heap of washers, dryers, and random junk. It was starting to look like Sanford and Son when Jerry asked in a polite sweet voice, "When are you going to turn in all this metal? It's really an eyesore."

I felt bad for how I had stacked up a 5 car garage worth of rusty metal. The Summit Police got involved because a different neighbor called me in. I agreed to turn the metal in load for load until everything was gone. It was starting to look like my days of junking were over before they had begun. That was until my mom called me at work at the thrift shop. She told me about a new franchise that was started in Milwaukee called 1-800-Got-Junk?. My mom spoke about the rags to riches story of fellow high school dropout Brian Scudamore. Brian had been in a McDonald's drive-thru and saw a beat-up old pickup truck, and instantly envisioned using the McDonald's franchise model to be the FedEx of junk removal. It was a story I could relate to because I was a high school dropout and the Got Junk? business model was to charge for rubbish, so it would let me make a livable wage for someone who suffers from type 1 bipolar disorder.

My mom called me again to tell me she put an ad on Craigslist. She put the name The Junk Truck as our business name. I smiled as I repeated the name to myself. Again, I was let out of my cage to make a beeline for Sparky.

My first job was for an office space that was renovating the walls. It was two huge rooms of cut up drywall sheets. I bid it at $250 (low ball) and hired one of the truck drivers at the thrift store, Jesus, to help me. If it was a normal estimate, I would have charged over $2,000, but I didn't do my homework, so I almost lost money. I didn't call the landfill to see how much they would charge, so I didn't know what to bid.

Our next job was another close disaster. Jesus and I went to a job in Richfield with a job that had about 50 yards worth of concrete. Not knowing about weight limits on a truck, I told the customer that I would load the concrete all the way to the top. Jesus kept advising against the idea because he said the truck won't be able to stop with a full load of broken concrete. Not wanting to disappoint the customer because I was a naive, stupid 19-year-old, I almost filled the concrete to the top. The worst part was we had to break up the concrete with a sledgehammer. It took most of the day to work hard, not smart, and Jesus eventually talked me into taking the customer's money and running for the hills.

We set out with our dangerously overweight load. Richfield is a very hilly part of Wisconsin, and as the GMC Sierra tried with all its might to make it up the hill, the truck would almost wheeze because of how out of breath it was. I was hauling this DOT violation nightmare up and around the Holy Hill area. On top of that, the truck was having a hard time stopping at intersections. I white-knuckled it home as Jesus kept saying how crazy it was that we were driving with this load. Jesus taught me that day about how much weight can go in a Junk Truck.

My first few calls after that for junk removal were around the area of Oconomowoc where I lived. My first client was a bankruptcy attorney that called me to get rid of a bunch of Amazon boxes. He had no time to go shopping, so he would order all of his household needs off of Amazon. This guy would open his garage, and it would be almost full of cardboard. My next client was out in Ixonia. This gentleman we will call Mr. Chicken. He was another craigslist find. Mr. Chicken was a very wealthy man who had a small shop in Ixonia that he ran an empire out of. He has 10 or 12 businesses, but his main business is a little sinister.

He runs a chicken slaughtering factory! Mr. Chicken discussed in detail how he slaughtered 350,000 chickens a day! First, the chickens are loaded on a truck. Then, the truck gets backed up on a tipping dock that dumps the chickens out onto a platform. Next, the chickens are grabbed by a machine by their feet and run through water with an electric current that knocks the cock unconscious. Then, the chickens get their throats slit by a blade and a machine rips all their feathers off their body. Lastly, they enter the filet phase where they are made into cuts for restaurants or grocery stores. Think about that the next time you are slamming Miller High Life at Buffalo Wild Wings.

The first time I met Mr. Chicken, I moved stuff out of an attic for him at his hideout. The space had a garage filled with expensive cars all with flat tires. He is the type of rich guy that doesn't value his possessions because he can always replace said item. Mr. Chicken lived in a house that literally looked like Tony Soprano's crib from the HBO crime drama. In spring and fall, he would have me haul his patio furniture to and from his house.

Whenever you talked to him, it was almost like he was in a business meeting somewhere else. He wore a headset and was actually pretty condescending. He treated my employees like peasants by not even acknowledging that they were human. For some reason, I really respect him to this day. Yes, Mr. Chicken does activities that I don't support, but that is his life choice in the end. I will not judge someone for messed up bullshit. I, too, make mistakes and do bad things, but I consider myself a good person who does bad from time to time. Mr. Chicken is a good person doing bad things. That is why I try not to judge people by their choices or actions. He is just another human being trying to provide for his family. I see people in grey. Not everyone is good or bad, but grey.

Our next Craigslist call would open my eyes to how horrifying junk removal work can be. I got a call from a contractor to clean up drywall in a basement from a burst water pipe. I knew my mom couldn't handle that type of work, so I asked my loser uncle Jared to help me load up.

It was on the North Side of Milwaukee in a ghetto neighborhood. The North Side of Milwaukee is very run down. Some of the houses are in ruins. The North Side is also riddled with crime and violence. The house we pulled up to was dilapidated. A red contractor van with a youthful 20-year-old kid was behind the wheel. He got out and led us down rickety old stairs to a basement with no working lights. The ceiling of drywall had fallen down from water damage and the gum board had turned into a crumbly paste.

We said we would shovel a full truck into the bed, but my unemployed loser uncle was already bitching. The basement was a moldy apocalypse and my uncle was going to bitch and moan the whole time about sitting in that humid, dark environment. I can still close my eyes and see my uncle Jared, in a respirator, scooping up stinky drywall. The ground had a puddle of water mixed with drywall to soak up the stale fluids. We spent the entire day shoveling moldy, drywall sludge. Because the drywall was wet, the load ended up looking like a big ball of wet toilet paper in the truck.

The worst part was the 20-year-old sat in his van and read a book. Come to find out the company was his daddy's business because he tried to short us on our full load price. The little bitch claimed that we didn't have a full load because it wasn't overflowing and falling out of the truck. My uncle in a rage spat out, "No, that is wet, heavy drywall; we absolutely need 350 dollars!"

Next, we got a job in Whitewater for a garage cleanup. The client opened the garage door and the guy had construction debris with a heaping pile of dirty diapers on top. I just remember putting my gloves on and saying, "A job is a job." My mom was my first employee, so she put on her gloves and we threw the doo-doo diapers in the truck. Even though I was a poop man, it felt good to finally have a purpose for my life.

Our next phase was to have the Oconomowoc Enterprise newspaper do a feature story on me. My mom wrote a press release and one day while working at the thrift store I got a call from the paper. They wanted to feature my junk business in both the Oconomowoc Enterprise and the Waukesha Freeman! The writer told me to drive the truck to the Enterprise Building on Wisconsin Avenue for an interview/photoshoot.

We showed up with the dirty diapers in the back of the truck for my big interview. They got my story down and took a few photos of me pretending to load my truck. It was a really cool moment in my life to be interviewed by the same newspaper I worked for as a young paperboy. It was special to see my name in print. To this day, I still keep newspaper clippings in a binder; I sometimes look at the pages when I am sad.

After the newspapers ran my story, I got over 100 calls from people who were inspired by the story of being a dropout turned junk man. A woman from Hartland called and said her son really liked the article and wanted to be my first real employee. I had a significant number of first employees that were just minute men. They were waiting for an incoming job, so having a mainstay employee would be a new experience for the both of us. I came to find out that he had special needs and was looking for a first job. I agreed to meet with him in Pewaukee. I didn't know much about hiring, so I knew he would be the right man for the job. We both didn't know about the workforce.

You're Hired!

Real Junk Truck review

Name Withheld ★★★★★ 3/11/2011

My friend recommended that I call The Junk Truck to remove my old appliances. She raved about their service and thought they were nice guys. Boy was she right. The guys were efficient and friendly. I also liked the fact that they were going to recycle my appliances to save me some money. I had a really good experience. I will recommend them to others.

We will call my newfound employee Mr. Good Guy for this part of the story. He was very kind with a gentle demeanor. Mr. Good Guy was a 15-year-old kid with a chubby build. In the haircut department, he was rocking a buzz cut with dirty blonde follicles. He was a happy guy that was excited to work at his first job. He didn't drive though, so he would need to be picked up. He lived in Hartland, so I would pick him up to go out and perform junk jobs.

On one occasion, we went to a house in Bay View. This is the area in Milwaukee where all the wannabe art snobs dwell. It is also where retired scene kids go to raise a family. A young guy had an old 1950s fridge in the basement. It was at the bottom of the stairs taunting us. I had worked at the thrift shop moving furniture, but the store was all one level, so I didn't have the manual on how to bring up a fridge safely. First, we were using the wrong dolly. Second, we had no strap to hold the fridge onto the dolly. Mr. Good Guy was on the bottom as I used the dolly to hump the fridge up the flight. We were taking the old fridge one stair at a time. We seemed to be making it! Suddenly, at the top, the fridge fell off the dolly and Mr. Good Guy went down with it. The fridge hit him on the leg but he was okay. The way the fridge fell I thought it would amputate his leg. The kid was very shaken but said he was alright. He lay on the ground in front of the customer and he had an "I just got bit by a dog" kind of look on his face. PURE SHOCK! I went and fetched a bungee from off the tarp of the truck.

We properly used a bungee for the tarp to use as a makeshift strap to hold the fridge tight and got it loaded into the truck. The customer said, "I am just glad no one got hurt". After that day, I wouldn't use the kid anymore because I thought he was a liability. Now in my 30's, I have reflected on the situation and know that I absolutely was the liability. I was very young and had no professional training. I had failed my first employee. Years later, I helped Mr. Good Guy (now a young man) get a job at Goodwill Industries. He got the job because of being involved with The Junk Truck in its early days in Wisconsin.

I still think about Mr. Good Guy. He was always in a very easygoing mode. He approached life with happiness. I think about that sometimes. I wish that I could go back to how easy life was back then. Just go pick someone up and make a few hundred in a few measly hours.

I majorly flubbed being a boss to Mr. Good Guy. It was a learning lesson moving forward. I was in a major bind because jobs were coming in at a rapid pace. My grandpa had remarried and the marriage brought along a 13-year-old boy. My grandpa and step-grandma suggested that I take the young lad with me on a job for a client in Brookfield. The city lies just outside of Milwaukee County. It is a rich suburb with doctors and lawyers resting their heads on their 100 dollar pillows. Mark was a 13-year-old who was very tall for his age, but he was extremely skinny. I really needed a hand moving these railroad ties for the client so I brought the underdeveloped boy to the job with me.

When I got to the house, an old woman with a thick German accent answered the door. I was dressed in my green polo with my fancy clipboard, but all the woman could do was stare at Mark. She then coldly said, "Do you really think that boy will be able to lift those railroad ties? He's just a child!"

Me drinking the 1-800-Got-Junk Kool-Aid, I assured her that he will be able to perform the task. If you know anything about railroad ties, they are dense wood. I mean for Christ's sake, trains drive over them. The little old lady then blurted out, "I used 1-800-Got-Junk once and they came with the truck three-quarters of the way full; I hope you will be able to finish the job. This kid won't make it! His muscles aren't developed enough!"

For some reason, I really thought that a 13-year-old could move railroad ties, but I was dead wrong! Mark struggled to lift them with me. Now the next part I'm not proud of, but I gave young Mark a really hard time for not being strong enough to lift the logs. I was a huge fucking asshole looking back. Another problem was the lady lived on an embankment, so we had to carry the railroad ties uphill. Mark would always let the railroad ties slip and I would be right there to fulfill my job of being a cousin fucker that would take my anger out on him. It was completely fucking wrong in the grand scheme of life. Looking back now in my 30's, I understand the value of money and no amount of money is worth putting someone down or walking all over someone. We are all humans who deserve to be treated at our jobs with kindness and always feel appreciated. In the end, young Mark turned out to be a kick-ass army sergeant. Mark could break my face by just blinking at me. He is a total Army badass now, so let that be a lesson to all the bosses out there: treat your employees with respect because they might grow up to be able to kill you.

Lady of Fear

Real Junk Truck review

Name Withheld ★★★★★ 8/20/2018

What a great service. These guys
were hard-working and honest. They
gave me a quote over the phone and
when they came out to remove my
items, it was actually less than the
original quote. How honest is that?
I love this company and will be
referring them to as many people as
possible. Thank You, Junk Truck!

I was still so new at running a business. I
was twenty and hungry, but very green. I had no
idea that the junk business would deal with very
touchy subjects. A lot of the business is dealing
with death or divorce. Some kind of drastic
change in someone's life is what spreads your
bread and butter for your business. I got a call for
a job in St. Francis which was all the way to the
lakefront of Lake Michigan. I didn't know if I
wanted to accept the job because of the distance
to the lakefront, but it was to be one of my first
cleanouts!

I needed an employee so I hired my Uncle
Jared to do this one-off job with me. Jared would
work six months, "just enough to qualify for
unemployment," then he would get fired somehow
to collect unemployment. Even though Jared did
drive, he insisted that I pick him up 25 minutes

away at his house in Sussex. What is it with all my employees needing to be picked up? Needless to say, he could use the money. I picked Jared up at his house and we headed for the lakefront.

When we arrived, the energy got sucked right out of me the moment that I saw the clients. It was an out-of-state couple. The wife's brother died and he was a hoarder. She couldn't even step inside the house without wanting to faint. She was really going through something. They immediately insulted me by saying, "Your truck looks really small." I would be a millionaire if I gave myself a nickel for every time that I heard, "That's it?" when a client saw my truck. I had to basically talk them into letting me do the job for them. They were unsure if I could clean the whole house out in one day with one truck and one Jared.

I was starting to wonder... Jared is a really lazy person with OCD, so a hoarding situation makes his brain melt. We went upstairs and started sifting through mounds of stuff in each room. I started to feel anxious and went from room to room trying to clear out the whole house in one handful. Jared was bitching and moaning as his OCD drove him through a wall. He grabbed a broom that was stuck to a bunch of junk and immediately broke down in anger. Everything needs to be tidy for Jared. We loaded up the first load and took it in to hand unload it at the dump. We came back for another. The woman of the deceased brother kept having nervous breakdowns by her husband's truck as we tossed in her dead brother's possessions. I didn't realize at the time that as she watched her brother's house get cleared out she was losing her brother with every item hauled off.

Load after load came out of the upstairs of the flat. While we were inside the dead brother's room, we found a complete, commemorative quarter set. It's funny how my brain can make me forget that we never handed his grieving sister that quarter set. Truthfully, I popped every quarter out its slot and cashed them in at a bank for a few hundred dollars. The dead brother had both the D and the P sets of quarters. That is a confession that I will have to live with. Anyway, we ended up almost clearing out the house in one day, and we promised to come back the next day (Sunday) to finish the job.

When we parked the truck for loading, we had to park in the neighbor's driveway a little bit. That day, a lot of construction crews were using the driveway, too. When I parked the Junk Truck, this old man came out and started screaming, "You bastard! You backed your truck up into my metal railing!" The funny thing is that I never felt the railing hit against my truck. No jerking forward or anything, so I couldn't have done the damage to the railing! Because I was a young kid, I apologized for something that I didn't do. I even promised to have it fixed but the old neighbor just threw up his hands and blurted, "Forget it."

Jared and I completed the cleanout and the couple was very pleased. The wife even said that she would tell her friends who lived in

Wisconsin to use The Junk Truck. A big part of junk removal is winning over a client. They start out thinking your truck is small and they end with thinking you didn't steal from them.

Load it Up!

Real Junk Truck review

Name Withheld ★★★★★ 2/9/2017

Highly recommend!! Trustworthy &
honest. They come, they pick up,
they do the lifting...easy peasy!!!

When you are young, people will take advantage of you at every chance they get. When you have youth, it's almost like you have a sign that says, "I'm young! Please lie to me and leave me in the dust." I was still getting the notches on my belt in terms of junk removal jobs. I was earning my stripes by doing any job that called my cell phone.

This guy called and said that his Dad was downsizing into a home. The guy said that he would pay the prices once explained over the phone. I had a minuteman situation going on when it came to junk removal employees. I had guys just waiting to suit up and show up when it was time for war. This time I used my buddy, Mokè.

Mokè was working at Arby's at the time, so he was really glad to have a side gig. We arrived in Hartland to find 3 middle-aged men that had gathered to help their dad downsize. There was a lot of stuff that needed to come out of the garage.

We loaded the first truckload and went to hand unload the truck at the dump.

When we came back, the boys decided to get rid of more stuff and wanted to load a whole second truck. I explained how I charged based on volume, so it would be another $425. The one son said, "We're already giving you $425! We will not pay for the next truck. Just as I'm about to call off the job, one of the sons holds up a kid's bike and says, "Where does this go, Paw?"

The old man in a weak voice said, "Throw it in the truck!"

I bit my lip in anger! These fucking assholes were walking all over me because I was young! Because I'm a pushover that couldn't say no at this point, I gladly accepted my 425 instead of 850. On the way home I had a complete rage at Mokè. He said, "Dude! You should just be glad you got, like, hundreds of dollars in 2 hours." I didn't know at the time how good I had it at that point.

Kevin Serone Era

Real Junk Truck review

Name Withheld ★★★★★ 8/6/2012
Scottsdale, AZ

Several trips to the basement were required to haul out several items, such as several desk parts, tables, and cabinets. Travis and his colleague were very pleasant as they made several trips out of the basement hauling several miscellaneous items. They worked quickly and were careful not to damage anything on their way out. We were fortunate enough to have a Junk Truck coupon to use at the time of payment. I would recommend Travis Geier and Josh to anyone that needed to have junk removed from their establishment. They worked hard and got the job done beyond satisfaction.

I needed someone who already kind of knew the moving trade. I was friends with a girl at the thrift store I worked at and she had mentioned her stoner boyfriend, Kevin, would be a great fit at The Junk Truck. She jotted his number down on a crumpled up piece of paper and said to call when a job came in.

I was hesitant to use Kevin because I knew he was a wild party animal, but in junk removal you end up using whoever because it's hard to find non-drug addicts to do the jobs.

I ended up using Kevin for a job and realized we worked really well together. He was really into doing designer rave drugs and going to rave parties. He had goopy, self-made dreadlocks. We would sometimes end a Junk Truck shift by sitting on couches in the back of the truck and getting high together. We were becoming fast friends and I was becoming better at the art of junk removal. I was being safer now that I knew the dangers. After what happened to Mr. Good Guy, I went through a few fill-ins, but I was ready to have someone full-time. Kevin was good at the moving aspect of junk removal, so we did really good work for people.

One good memory with Kevin was when we picked up a Hoveround wheelchair from a customer. Yes, it is the same wheelchair from the commercial where geriatric folks are cruising around the Grand Canyon in their electric wheelchairs. Afterwards, we got so stoned back at my parent's and drove the thing around my yard. Kevin wanted to take it to a party, so I gave it to him. He told me they did ecstasy and drove girls around on his lap at the party. Because we had no charger, the Hoveround stopped working eventually.

As time went on, Kevin started to attend more and more rave parties. He was helping run the lasers and lights for DJs, experimenting more with drugs, and becoming a little removed from reality. This led to him becoming more careless at The Junk Truck. Kevin would drive to Chicago to run the lasers for the party. He would stay up all night doing designer drugs, then he would come back and work for The Junk Truck. It was starting to become an issue, but it is so hard to keep people in junk removal because the people who want to work for you are usually drug addicts. Your talent pool for junk removal is usually plagued with either convicted felons or drug addicts; this means you have to look the other way when in the hiring process. In the tenure of the company, I had four different people work for me that had a felony for stabbing someone, so Kevin to me was solid because he wasn't a violent criminal. Kevin was someone I called a friend. Sadly, it was going to be hard to let Kevin go.

Kevin was always high now. He started making a fair amount of mistakes that I always paid for. We were moving a fridge for a guy with a spiral stair set that led out of the basement. The fridge would have to be lifted straight up the stairs and twisted around the curve of the stair set. The homeowner was a guy in his early thirties and he was really happy to hire us because of how hard it was going to be to twist the fridge out. There was one problem: they had a window at the stairs' turn. It would be difficult to not break the window.

We tried several times to lift the fridge out and do the twist, but each time we would come close to the window. I told Kevin on one attempt, "If

you twist the fridge, you will break the window."
The next move Kevin does is do a twist with the
fridge. BANG! The window is broken!

The homeowner says right away, "Don't
worry about it." We get the fridge to the truck, lift it
up, and close the gates. The homeowner says, "So
how do we pay for this window?" I told him we
would be in touch because I would get a few
quotes for him. We eventually got the window
fixed, but I was a little mad at Kevin for being so
careless. I was mad at him inside, but accidents
happen... or do they? Even though Kevin broke
the window, it seemed like Kevin would still be a
good fit for a while; that was until I got my big
break on the radio...

Methadone Killed the Radio Star

Real Junk Truck review

Name Withheld ★★★★★ 2/7/2012
Wauwatosa, WI

Travis and his assistant removed 42 years' worth of accumulation, including a freezer, from our basement. They arrived on time (actually a few minutes early) and were very professional. They were very careful to make sure that they didn't damage doors, windows, etc. Very polite and pleasant.

The Junk Truck was doing really good business at this point. I had started by riding my bicycle around town to pass flyers out and ended up having enough money to advertise on the radio. The thrift store manager came to me and said, "Travis, you are always doing junk jobs now, so we think it is time to part ways. We need someone to be here through the week." It was a good feeling to be transitioning to being a full-time entrepreneur. It was time to step it up a notch with the business.

My mom's friend worked in radio ad sales and sold me on a package that would involve a morning show host endorsing The Junk Truck. I won't name this person out of protection for her career. The morning host, who shall not be named, was going to tear out her drywall and we would haul it away. Wisconsin radio is very corny and predictable, so this particular host's morning show was in that vein. Her show was meant for middle-aged women who were grasping on to their past youth. The show was filled with a lot of gameshow-type segments and uninteresting facts. She also had a very thick Wisconsin accent. The host was very excited to have us do the job because she had just bought her first home. Seemed fucking simple, right? Fucking wrong! I had a weird feeling my big break would end in disaster.

The night before, I had two people in mind to help me with this big job for radio endorsement. One was a drunk named Nate Schwantz and the other was molly-poppin', methadone-munching Kevin. At the last minute, I trusted Kevin to help me, but Kevin was dating a heroin addict from Delafield. Little did I know, they hadn't slept at all. They stayed up doing Methadone all night long. Kevin almost didn't answer his phone that morning. I met up with him at the BP gas station in Delafield. The moment he hopped in, I noticed his eyes were glazed red. I just thought that Kevin smoked a little marijuana, but he kept babbling about nothing and was being more belligerent than normal. I was naive to the fact that he was on Methadone. We got close to where this nameless morning show host lived and parked to meet her outside. She lived in a nicer part of Milwaukee. Old well kept houses from Milwaukee's yesteryear. It was definitely a place to raise a family in the city.

Immediately, when Kevin stepped out of the truck, I noticed he was in flip-flops. With this being basically a construction site, I immediately grabbed a pair of water boots that I kept in the truck, but it was too late. The radio host saw Kevin in sandals and was horrified. Haha, her first impression of us was her questioning where his work boots were. She even blurted, "He has boots, right?"

The radio host hesitantly showed us the piles of drywall, and they were massive piles I wouldn't be able to move in one day. She must have torn out all the drywall in her whole house! The drywall was that old school stuff that crumbles like hard rocks. It would be impossible to do this job without a machine. Not to mention Kevin's current state of being.

High on heroin, Kevin started to rake up the drywall chunks still in his sandals. Kevin came with no boots to a job site; he was in too much of a hurry to grab boots because he had been up all night doing methadone with his girlfriend. He would stand at the top of the pile, in his sandals, and try to get the crumbles of drywall into a wheel barrel. I eventually got Kevin to put the water boots on his feet.

She came to check on Kevin to make sure he wasn't dead, and instead, Kevin inserted himself into a conversation about radio. He informed the radio host that her morning show sucked and that Kramp and Adler were better than her. At this moment, I wanted to evaporate into thin air. The radio host was nice and kindly stated that Kramp and Adler were for a male demographic in their 20's and 30's. Kevin replied again, "Nah, Kramp and Adler are actually funnier than you."

Because of Kevin being on Methadone and the drywall being crumbled chunks, it took us forever to even load a quarter of the truck up. I ended up telling the radio host that we were going to take what we had. By this point, she was scared of Kevin because he was belligerently shouting obscenities. He kept calling the host a bitch. I was in survival mode at this point. I just have to muscle through this.

As we packed up, she was standing by the street with her husband consoling her. I walked up and started to cry. I told the radio host that this was the most embarrassing moment of my life. She put on a fake smile and said it would be okay. We got in the truck and Kevin commented, "That lady was a bitch!" I just stayed silent at the landfill. I was in pain, but we had to unload the drywall. My truck didn't have a dump, so we had to unload it by hand. The first thing Kevin did is grab a huge chunk of drywall and throw it over the truck's windshield, shattering it. I screamed at him as big machines trudged through the garbage around us.

I took Kevin home and didn't speak to him until years later. I forgave him because I understand addiction and mental illness, but it took years for me to be at that point with him. Kevin is now a big-time insurance adjuster that travels the country. He has completely turned his life around.

Quiznos

Real Junk Truck review

Name Withheld ★★★★★ 7/14/2012
Wauwatosa, WI

Hauled off construction debris and
landscaping stones. Great job! Nice
guys. Would use them again!

The drunk that I was supposed to use on
the methadone radio gig, I met in line ordering a
Quiznos sandwich. I liked the look of Nate
Schwantz. He reminded me of stoners from my
hometown. He worked at Quiznos. I ordered him to
make a honey mustard chicken and by the time it
popped out the other side of the oven, Nate was
hired at The Junk Truck. We started smoking weed
together. One day, he told me his name was Nate
Schwantz and my eyes bulged out of their sockets.
I asked, "Is your dad Ned Schwantz?"

Nate nervously answered, "Yes, he is..."

"Dude! Your dad was my childhood
counselor that got me diagnosed as bipolar!" I felt
like I was in the presence of royalty! Nate's dad
sent me away to a mental hospital when I was 12. I
got bullied at school, so I planned to go to school
and murder my bully. I was forced by Nate's dad
to go stay at Milwaukee Psych, and I had to miss
my 8th-grade science egg drop! What a fucking
world!

Nate was in a rebuilding phase of his life because of a felony drug charge, so he was living in a studio in Oconomowoc. Not long afterwards, he moved almost 25 minutes away to Merton. This was a problem because Nate liked to get blackout drunk every night. It almost ran like clockwork: Nate would drink all night, then pass out, and I would be twiddling my thumbs waiting for him by the truck that morning.

I would always end up calling him and the phone call would usually go like this, "Hello" (sleepyhead voice).

"Nate, where are you? The job is at 8! It's now 8:25!"

"I will be there soon; just let me put pants on!"

The issue with firing Nate was that we were becoming fast friends. He ended up getting a DUI and was placed on that alcohol ankle bracelet.

I got a call from a young up-and-coming remodeler who wanted to try out The Junk Truck. The guy was very worried about cost, but he had a new worry when Nate and I showed up to haul the crap away. Nate chose to wear shorts that day, exposing his ankle bracelet to the fucking world.

The guy immediately asked Nate, "Are you a registered sex offender?"

Nate smiled and said, "No, it is for alcohol monitoring." I saw the client's eyes get relieved a touch, but was still seeing us as drunk losers now. The client asked me about how we made a profit, so I explained how the loads work.

He replied, "How do you guys even make money then?" I honestly questioned that, too.

On another morning, I was waiting at the truck for Nate and ended up calling his roommates to wake him up. Nate was mumbling and singing in a loud voice in the background as his roommates became frustrated at Nate for being incompetent to The Junk Truck.

Most junk removal companies become taxis to their troubled employees. The burnout employees know you need them, so you end up picking up and dropping off all your employees. Nate was a little different because he did have a car, but it was better for you to go get him with your car because he would always be out late the night before.

Turd

Real Junk Truck review

Name Withheld ★★★★★ 8/30/2017

What an efficient working group. I hired them to clean out the useless items in my basement and garage that I stored for far too long. They did an amazing job getting some of the heavy items out. I was impressed and will use them again!

Very early on, I realized just what an impact junk removal had on the disabled. I had no idea part of my job would be helping people through tough situations. Over the years, I have had customers cry on my shoulder because of what The Junk Truck provided for their families. As I write this I am a 33-year-old, fat drug addict, and totally broke. If all I ever have is the memories of helping people, that's totally fine by me.

One of my favorite memories of helping someone in need was for a blind man whose wife was a hoarder. The wife was in the hospital, so we needed to clean the space out so this blind man wouldn't trip over piles of junk! There was a counselor involved, and she brought us to a basement that was covered in a layer of cat hair. There was too much stuff for a guy with just one Junk Truck and one lazy employee that was the second hire straight out of Quiznos.

While we were in the basement, it was a little hysteria to try and help this guy. The counselor wanted a chair to go that was covered in cat hair. We were walking on a layer of papers and assorted junk. We grabbed the stuffed chair and a cat jolted out from underneath. I watched the cat run away, and it had turds knotted into it near its anus. There were dingleberries just hanging off the cat!

The lazy Quiznos worker was freaking out and wanted to leave. I didn't blame him. We got into the truck when it was full and went to dump the load.

This was in the semi-early days of GPS and I had an archaic Tom-Tom device that looked like an XM satellite radio. The Tom-Tom kept giving us the business because the fucker was sending us in circles. I had a complete temper tantrum in the truck in front of Quiznos 2 and he was annoyed. I was slamming my fists into the steering wheel and screaming, "Why won't it fucking work!"

The scared employee replied, "Dude, you should just know where you're going!"

We dumped and returned for another load, but we ended the day after that. We never got called back because The Junk Truck was too small of a company, but I became conscious of the fact that this business would make a difference to the community of Southeastern Wisconsin.

Porno Removal with Travis

Real Junk Truck Review

Name Withheld ★★★★★ 7/6/2012
Midway, AR

Travis Geier was very courteous and helpful. On the same day, I called in 100 degrees he and his helper came to our house to haul away my items. Excellent job by both of them in tough circumstances with the heatwave. Would call them anytime for help in the future and highly recommend them to anyone.

The company was starting to get notoriety and jobs. One day, I got a call from a subcontractor. He said, "I have a really weird job for you guys."

At this point, I had seen dirty diapers, and dingleberries so I said, "We have probably seen worse."

He laughed, and said, "Just wait until you see this condo." I booked the appointment for a few days out and when the day came, the subcontractor called to ask me if I would pretend like I have known him for years in front of the client. I agreed. Coming from a family of criminals,

49

I did not give a fuck about pretending to have known him for years.

We pulled up to these ugly brown condominiums in Brown Deer. The city is a rough area; filled with crime. I was horrified at what would be inside this condo. We found the contractor's van and pulled up to find the unit. We met the client, who is the brother of the person who owns the condo. As the subcontractor was flipping through the keys, he informed us that there has been no electricity or running water in the condo for 5 years.

He opened the door and sunshine filled the space where shadows once were. I was stunned at what I saw inside the house. There were huge piles in every room like a hoarder, but there was a distinction in the hoarder's possessions. The only items in these heaping piles of trash were hostess cupcakes, bondage porn, and brand new women's clothes in the packaging. This pervert had porn in the media form of magazines, VHS, and magazines of women wrestling topless.

They left us alone to clean up this porn apocalypse. We put the truck next to the house and started tossing junk out the window. We found a lot of pot paraphernalia around. I found a Graffix bong where the bong water was so dirty that it had turned to a black sludge in the chamber. Nate found a series of polaroids on the ground. We looked through them one by one. The first few photos were of a fat man we presumed to be the dying owner of this sex dungeon. When we got to the last Polaroid in the series, it was a picture of the fat man holding his penis in his hand. Nate threw the photos on the ground instantly as we scrounged for more bondage porn magazines to fill the truck.

The first load out of that condo was entirely made up of bondage porn and women's wrestling topless mags. I still have a vivid memory of looking down at the truck through the window and my massive stake bed truck filled to the brim with creepy, violent porn. I didn't know where to dump a whole load of bondage porn, so we sadly dumped the first load in the dump.

We got back and started to fill the truck with more porn, hostess cupcakes, and women's clothes. We were wondering what was up with the women's clothes when my friend found the guy's phone records. We put two and two together and realized the guy was calling 900 sex hotlines and asking the women their size and then ordering the call girls clothes from Talbot's Fashion Catalogue. The call girls probably refused to accept the clothes, leaving him with a hoarder's house full of stitchings.

The condo itself was disgusting. It had a brown shag carpet with food particles in it, the walls had slime on them, and the toilet was growing white crystals out of it that resembled a crack rock.

We were cleaning out the kitchen cabinets, but instead of canned food, there were pre-recorded VHS tapes lining the cabinets. Part of me wanted to know what was on those tapes, but the other part of me kept filling them up in the yellow, plastic garbage cans.

Nate was in the master bedroom when he found a Chinese finger trap type box. Instead of trying to figure out the combination, we set the box on the ground and stomped it with our feet, expecting to find rare coins. What was inside the box was a school picture of what looked to be an 8-year-old girl and a human's tooth!

Years later, I told that story to my improv troupe and someone pointed out there was probably some child porn or illegal sex acts on those pre-recorded VHS tapes, but it made for a great comedy opening.

We were informed by the brother that the owner was on his death bed in the hospital and he wanted to keep this clean-out hush-hush. Being 20 at the time, I wasn't picking up what was the reality of this situation. A few months later, Nate and I were smoking with some people and he brought up the job with a group of friends. Nate laughed and said, "You've never done porno removal with Travis?"

Perfect OSHA Practices

Real Junk Truck Review

Name Withheld ★★★★★ 2/3/2018

Anticipating a move to another house, I had this company come out three different times- the last time to take everything down from the rafters of the garage, a chore I was glad to hand off to someone else. Each time I dealt with The Junk Truck, I found them responsive, on time, and polite. The team always made fast work of the pick-up, even sweeping up part of my garage. Highly recommended!

Needless to say that OSHA wasn't visiting us at The Junk Truck. When I started, I didn't know anything about safety, how much weight could go in a truck, or the right steps to keep workers safe. I was basically a 19-year-old burnout with a truck when I started.

I would say the heaviest item we ever lifted was with Nate Schwantz. We pulled up to a repeat customer's driveway. On the edge of the asphalt sat the heaviest steel and concrete gun case. The customer was like, "I know you can get this in the truck, Travis!" I died inside a little because we didn't have a lift to get this safely up on the bed of the truck. The customer peeled me off a check and literally left the scene of the crime.

The back of the Junk Truck had wooden gates that came off. We cleared a little out of the back to be able to fit this monster in. Nate started to bitch because of how crazy this was to attempt to put in the truck without a lift. I was an absolute idiot and just joked it off that we would get it in. We tipped the gun safe on the back of the bed and started to try to lift this thing.

Nate Schwantz was a really strong guy, so as we lifted it, I could see all his veins shooting out of his arms. We were grunting and groaning while we struggled to not become paralyzed. We had the gun safe in parallel with the truck now, but we needed to stand it up to be in the truck. We had to lift it over our heads to have it stand up.

Nate and I had it over our heads as we saw our life flash before our eyes. We stood it up! Nate was like, "Let's just go."

We ended up driving the gun safe to Miller Compressing to recycle. When we weighed out, Nate informed me that the ticket read that the gun safe was 800 pounds. That meant that we lifted 400 pounds each! That was definitely a lesson in how much a mover can lift. We should have stayed away from that job! I was a dumbass like usual to accept that job.

Nate and The Wailers

Real Junk Truck Review

Name Withheld ★★★★★ 2/23/2018

They were great. They came on time and worked very hard. I didn't even have to organize all of the junk I wanted them to remove. They went on all levels to get the stuff out. Some of the furniture was extremely heavy which didn't seem to faze these guys. I was highly impressed with the guys and the company.

I wanted to do an outing with Nate because we were becoming fast friends. The first hang out for me and Nate was at a Milwaukee Brewers Game. My rep Pete Schlosser had given me tickets behind the home plate. I met Pete Schlosser by riding my bicycle and passing out fliers. He received one and saw something in me as a young entrepreneur. He took me under his wing and treated me like I was family. I still respect Pete Schlosser so much. He taught me business and marketing. These were the best seats I have ever gotten for a sporting event. I felt like such a businessman being offered free tickets because I was such an important client to Pete.

My happiness soured into misery from the moment we started to tailgate. Nate drank an ungodly amount of beer before the game. He was in stumble mode as we made our way to the seats.

Nate just kept screaming belligerent obscenities that made absolutely no fucking sense. I steered him into our seats and the view from Miller Park was breathtaking. Pete had asked that we be on our best behavior because everyone that sat around us was season ticket holders that all knew each other. Nate was anything but on his best behavior. He kept screaming, "Swing, batter batter!" Then Nate would put two fingers in his mouth and make a blood-curdling whistling sound. I was trying to get Nate to calm down, but he would just keep doing this annoying whistle that made heads turn.

I was so fucking embarrassed that I finally had been schmoozed into going to a game and now Nate was whistling so loud that it hurt your ears. We ended up leaving the game early because of Nate's shenanigans.

You would think I had learned my lesson not to take Nate anywhere, but up next was our trip to Summerfest. It is the world's largest music festival that no one has ever heard of. It is 11 days of people walking around wasted to catch their favorite county fair band. Summerfest is nicknamed, "Stumble Fest" because of how drunk people get at the festival. Nate was about to take that name to a whole different level. Bob Marley's original band, The Wailers, was playing one of the nights at the world's largest music festival. Nate was very pumped to go down to catch their set.

Summerfest works with advertisers to offer enticements to get you into the music fest by buying one of their products. This particular year, Miller Brewing was offering a free ticket with every purchase of a 24 pack of Miller Lite. I haven't drank since I was 20, I won't even drink kombucha, the plan was to just buy a 24 pack and never drink the beer.

Nate said, "I will drink the beer for us to get the free tickets for tonight!"

I remember thinking, "We just need the code inside the box; fuck the beer!"

Nate wanted to drive his '90s Chevy Lumina down to the lakefront, so we met at his grandma's where he was staying. He handed me his keys and mentioned, "Don't let me drive tonight. I am giving you these keys so I don't drive." He wanted me to drive so he could finish the 24 pack. That should have been my first sign to not go. Who the fuck drinks 24 beers in a 30-minute drive from Oconomowoc to Milwaukee? We headed out on I-94 towards the city; meanwhile, Nate started to slam beer after beer!

I kept asking, "Nate you're not going to finish all those beers by the time we get to Milwaukee are you?"

He looked at me and stated, "I will finish all 24 beers by the time we park."

Part of me should have known that no human drinks 24 beers in a half-hour's time, but

Nate was getting close to slamming the whole 24 pack. Nate didn't want to pay for parking, so we parked far away by the Amtrak Station. As we stepped out to stretch, Nate still had like 3 or 4 beers left. I said, "Fuck the beer; let's ditch the beer and head in!" Nate refused to go in until the entire 24 pack was finished. As we walked the good distance to Summerfest, Nate slammed the last 3 cans. This is the point where Nate started to act very strangely. He was definitely in a blackout state even before entering the Summerfest Grounds.

Again, I had to steer Nate into the Summerfest Grounds. The second we stepped inside, Nate walked up to a beer stand and ordered 2 more beers for himself. I shouted at Nate. "Dude, you already drank 24 beers before we got here! Are you going to be alive after drinking 2 more beers? That will be 26 beers, dude!" Nate grumbled that he would be fine.

Nate wasn't fine at this point. Nate was stumbling so bad that he looked like a zombie out of Night Of The Living Dead. For some reason, my mother was at Summerfest that day and wanted to meet up with me. The second we saw my mom by the rocks, my mom took one look at Nate and questioned, "Is he going to be okay?" I filled my mom in on how many beers Nate consumed. She kept begging Nate to just drink some water. All I wanted to do was spend time with my mom at the lakefront, but I had to play babysitter to old Hank Williams over here.

While I was talking to my mom, Nate had drifted off, so we parted ways to go look for him. I found Nate at a beer stand ordering 4 more beers! This is when I got fucking pissed off. I shouted, "Who the fuck are those beers for?" Nate was talking in a brand new language after having ordered his 29th beer for the night! Nate slammed all 4 beers making it to number 29.

It was starting to get dark and The Wailers were going to take the stage at 10:00. Nate and I headed to the stage, but Nate decided to run into the crowd without even looking if I was behind him keeping up. I saw Nate run into the crowd, and I said, "Fuck his drunk ass." I ended up just hanging out around the Fox 6 News van that was parked outside the stage area.

I called my mom and she met up with me to comfort me while Nate was destroying our second night out. My mom asked, "What are you going to do with Nate's car? I am worried that he won't be able to find his way back to the Amtrak Station."

My mom promised to stick around the Summerfest Grounds in case I would need a ride home. I told her that Nate had given me the keys to his Chevy Lumina. My mom made me promise that I wouldn't wait for drunk Nate because she didn't think he even knew who he was at this point. I missed the entire Wailers show because my mom and I just spent time together at the Lakefront. After the Wailers played their last note, I situated myself in front of the Fox 6 News Van again. I was sure Nate would see me because the van was literally parked dead center at the exit.

Suddenly, I got a call from Nate, "Where are you at, man?!?!?"

"Nate, I am standing in front of the Fox 6 News van." CLICK.

Suddenly I got another call from Nate, so I answered, "Where ya at, man?!?!?"

"Again, I am right outside by the Fox 6 News van. Where are you?" CLICK.

This was the second fucking time Nate had hung up on me. I just wanted to head back to Oconomowoc, but because Nate was belligerently drunk, I was being held hostage by his Chevy Lumina. I kept calling and Nate would answer, "Where are ya at bro?"

"I am by your car now. Nate, are you going to make it back here safely?" Nate hung up for a third time. I was basically on the side of the road staring at his crappy Chevy Lumina. The phone rang and I answered, "Nate, where the fuck are you?"

Nate replied, "I'm driving!"

I calmly answer, "Nate, how are you driving when I am staring at your fucking car!"

Nate hangs up again, so I dial again.

"Hey."

"Where the fuck are you, Nate?"

"I'm driving, bitch!"

I hung the phone up in anger. I called my mom to ask what to do. I wanted to wait for Nate, but my mom kept saying, "Nate isn't even in reality after his 29th beer. Just drive his car back to his grandma's and head to your apartment."

I got in the Lumina and headed back in Nate's car without him. I quickly parked it in the driveway of his grandma's. The next week, Nate refused to talk to me about leaving him in Milwaukee. His mother reached out to my mother and gave her her number for me to call. I called Nate's mom and she basically filled in the blanks about what Nate's night was like.

She said, "The police found Nate sleeping on a bench outside of a Pick N Save grocery store in Greenfield." I was stunned because Greenfield is near Milwaukee, but you would have to get on the freeway to reach Greenfield. How did Nate get 5 or 6 miles away from the Summerfest Grounds? His mom told me that she would convince Nate to reach out to me. His mom thanked me and said that I made the right decision to leave Nate in Milwaukee.

Nate was on probation, but the police said they wouldn't file the charge because they knew he needed to get help. Nate called later that week to apologize for his actions. I asked how he made it to Greenfield and he thought that he might have gotten in a car with a stranger. That was the last outing for The Junk Truck for a little while...

A Follicle Off Main

Real Junk Truck Review

Name Withheld ★★★★★ 8/11/2010
Milwaukee, WI

Removed two freezers and a
refrigerator from the basement. Was
only 165.00 but there is a $20 freon
charge per appliance.

They were here when promised. They
removed the door needed for room and
put it back on. Very careful and
concerned to not scratch, damage
anything while removing. Very
polite. The price was very
reasonable in comparison.

My first experience with an extreme
hoarder wasn't from the television program; it was
in a town called Watertown. The town is very blue-
collar and if you look at someone wrong you will
be lynched for being an Oconomowoc city slicker.
The city has old big buildings; a lot of very cute
corner brick buildings on every corner of
downtown. This makes the apartments upstairs to
be pretty decently sized.

I was called by a hairdresser who owned
the building and had an apartment unit upstairs
that needed cleaning out. Below was a hair cutting
salon; upstairs was a tremendous hoarding
situation.

I brought Nate Schwantz to the first pickup at the location. It was located on Market Street. We were parking the Junk Truck at around 9:00 AM when we saw 3 individuals walking toward us.

Two Caucasian town drunks were walking with an African American woman. They all looked like they slept on the streets, and the female was carrying a 12-pack of Pabst Blue Ribbon. They were just walking around with open intoxicants, in a small town, at 9 in the morning! Nate and I laughed so hard at these people not giving one fuck!

We finally meet the hairdresser outside after the bum situation, and she takes us upstairs to a very tiny hallway leading to two apartments. She opened the door to unit 2 and I was flabbergasted to see what was inside.

It was a very big apartment filled top to bottom with just rubbish. . ... I actually could climb piles of junk like mountains. Because of how high the junk and ceilings were, Nate and I were astonished at the sight of all this, but we started loading with high anxiety.

We didn't really know where to start, so we started off a little scatterbrained just grabbing different junk in all different rooms.

We were in a bedroom when I found a mixing bowl that had the batter and mixing spoon still in it. The batter had solidified to a concrete consistency. It was so strange because it was like the woman was mixing batter to bake a cake and then she just decided a cake wasn't on the menu for dinner tonight and just tossed it. Next, we found a plate full of chicken bones that were turning black.

This type of hoarding is what I would call filthy hoarding. This form of hoarding is the subculture where people live with rotting food, moldy furniture, and live in dusty conditions. Some folks can be neat hoarders, too. These hoarders just have so much stuff; I have seen neat hoarders organize their junk by attaching it with wire to the rafters in the garage. On that particular neat hoarding job we sat and clipped down every wired item for hours.

The hoarding tenants were a mother and a young daughter. They had lived there a decade and suddenly split only to leave the landlord for the removal bill. The hairdresser was honestly amazed they had accumulated so much stuff that there were paths between what I would call trash mountains. The piles were filled with garbage: old dirty papers, food, and lots of broken kids toys. It was sad to see how a child was living.

We could only do one load that day because it was a Saturday and the dumps close early. The next time we came back, I was with my friend, B. We ended up finding a bloody tampon in one of the piles of rubbish. We were disgusted by the bloody tampon, but you become numb to the grime in junk removal. You learn to just hold your breath and stuff the tampon in the bag. I only had one truck, so we only took four loads out of the house, and then the hoarding mansion's trail went cold. A year later, I got a really sweet letter from the hairdresser explaining all this, and the apartment was for rent, but I still lived at my apartment above Breakshots and did not want to move all of my belongings.

The Cover-Up

Real Junk Truck Review

Name Withheld ★★★★★ 9/28/2012
Shorewood, WI

Removed junk from the basement and garage. Workers were polite and efficient.

Life can truly be beautiful as you gaze upon moments in the past. In the beginning of the company, I did a lot of guerrilla marketing. That means that I put out yard signs, pass out fliers, or I would hold up a sign at a busy intersection.

I had a sign made for The Junk Truck and I planned on doing waves to cars passing by. My mom told me that she would go with me to hold a sign and wave.

It was a beautiful, sunny day, and my mom and I went and parked our car at Goerke's Corners in Brookfield. There is a 4-way intersection there with a lot of traffic whizzing by.

The sign was made out of a plastic-like fabric so we couldn't keep it straight (design flaw on my part). My mother and I tried our best to keep it straight as we jumped up and down, waving our hands, and shouting, "Call The Junk Truck!" I can still see us waving and jumping as cars flew past.

Some even honked at us and smiled. The memory is burned in my brain because that was before all the hurt and pain that would divide my mother and I's relationship years later....

If I was Brian Scudamore, of 1-800-Got-Junk fame, I would talk of the positives of guerilla marketing, but this is me, the piece of shit, so we will discuss the negatives.

My mom had let me borrow her Acura MDX to drive around and put yard signs off freeways, streets, and corners. I went down Pilgrim road in Brookfield, stopping, and putting yard signs out at every street light. At one of my usual spots, I pulled over to get the sign out. I walked with the sign and stabbed it into the ground. Across the street was a road construction crew that was trimming trees.

The moment the sign stabbed the ground a worker yelled out, "HEY! Get that shit outta here!" I turned around and gave him the finger, pulled my sign up, and loaded it back in the MDX. As I pulled away there was a stop sign. The worker, in a rage, approached my vehicle and put his head in the SUV. I grabbed Oasis' What's the Story Morning Glory on Compact Disc and pelted the case at his face. I sped away, but the asshole radioed to his buddy who was the flagger. The flagger thought he would play hero and step in the middle of the road, so I sped up to mow him down. He jumped out of the way like a stunt man in a movie. I giggled to myself as I sped into Menomonee Falls.

I didn't even make it back to my apartment above the bar before my mom was calling screaming bloody murder. My mom hissed through the phone, "What the fuck have you done? Four or 5 people reported you to the police for that fucking stunt you just pulled! They are investigating, Travis. You better save for a lawyer." I turned into a child who just hurt his friend. I told my mom to lie if she had to get me out of this. I sat in my apartment and fried my brain by smoking K2 to try and forget about my newly earned legal troubles.

The Brookfield detective was not going to let me get away with this psychotic bipolar stunt that I just pulled. I spent the next 2 weeks dodging detectives who were out for my blood. My mom had to speak with the detectives several times. My mom made up a story that she hired illegal immigrants at the t-shirt business that my mom and stepdad pretended to run. The detectives did not believe my mom would not know who was driving her own car, but this was another butt plug up their rectums that would prohibit them from shitting all over me in court. Because my mom claimed to not know who was driving, they couldn't necessarily pinpoint me as a sure driver of the MDX.

Another problem was that when the witnesses were shown a police lineup with my picture in the book along with others, the witnesses could never say for sure that the picture the cops showed them was really me. My appearance always changes; one minute I'm fat with long hair, the next I'm bald and skinny. That ended up being a roadblock for the detectives who could only charge me with a minor offense. I did end up hiring my defense attorney, Joseph Dorolack. He wanted me to keep fighting because he said the detectives could not prove that it was me driving. His legal advice though was simple, "Travis, you already have a number of disorderly conducts, what is one more on your record going to do?" So I added another charge to the pile.

Best Fucking Friends

Real Junk Truck Review

Name Withheld ★★★★★ 5/10/2012
Albuquerque, NM

Removal of miscellaneous items,
cardboard, boxes of "stuff" junk,
and trash from garbage. Basement and
one interior room, loading of truck
and hauling away appropriate items
to be recycled or donated.

Travis and Calvin were outstanding!
Travis responded promptly to my
email inquiry and answered questions
well. Their emphasis on donating and
recycling what can be reused or
recycled was evident and important
to me. Travis called again to
confirm the appointment and arrived
a little early. Travis gave me a
quote and when I accepted that, got
right to work. He packed the truck
tightly so as to reduce the cost.
They both worked very hard for over
two hours neatly sorting and loading
the truck. They were cheerful and
professional and also very very
careful as they removed the items
from my garage and basement and one
room inside. I couldn't be happier
with how pleasant they were, how
careful, and how hard they worked!
The price beat the competition by a
long shot and their emphasis on

recycling or donating was clear.
They were both very conscientious
and professional.

One of my best friendships blossomed
from The Junk Truck. Our friendship took place by
chance. I was around 22 or 23 years old, and most
of my friends moved out to the East Side of
Milwaukee. I was still living in my hometown of
Oconomowoc. A buddy of mine was living in a flat
in Milwaukee in the Riverwest neighborhood with a
gentleman named Calvin White. Calvin was a
shorter guy, loved heavy metal, and loved to
drink/smoke. I would hear people speak of Calvin,
and I secretly thought he was really cool, but I had
only met him a few times.

My buddy begged me to drive the Junk
Truck out to him and Calvin's flat in the Riverwest
neighborhood of Milwaukee. This same buddy
had promised to help me do a job on the East Side
that next morning, so I figured it would be nice to
wake up close to the job. I headed out to him and
Calvin's flat for the night. I backed the big, green
truck in their driveway.

That night, my buddy, who was supposed
to help, ended up getting smashed and fucking a
girl all night. My buddy's crackhead friend was
also crashing for the night, so I laid in a sleeping
bag listening to a girl moaning the words, "Fuck
me harder." Every so often you would hear my
buddy spank this brunette's ass. As I listened to
her have an orgasm, I was thinking to myself,

"Why am I 23 and sleeping on a friend's floor?" I barely slept that whole night.

In the morning, I banged on my buddy's door and he was still half in the bag. My friend rolled over and mumbled, "I am too hungover to work, so take Calvin with you."

I literally walked to Calvin's room and started shaking him violently. I noticed a pair of boots next to his bed, so I grabbed them, and said, "Calvin, wake up because we have a junk job to go to." Calvin was red in the face from drinking the night before, but he hopped right up. He booted up and we took off in the Junk Truck.

We arrived at an apartment complex on the East Side. The manager was an extremely spunky, kind lady that was super psyched that this service even existed. She wanted us to pull in the back, but I was unsure if the truck would get stuck back there. The narrow driveway was on the side of the building and made a sharp left to some garages at the back. There were tenants constantly coming and going so we decided to place the truck in the back. The lady had a big pile waiting in the back for us that tenants had left behind. We loaded up the junk and the lady praised us for being available on a Saturday. As we tried to make the left now right turn. I noticed my truck wheel wouldn't make the radius to get out of the back of the building.

My new employee, Calvin, watched as I kept almost demolishing the neighbor's fence to get out. We kept trying to line the truck up to get out, but it wouldn't work unless we scraped the side of the truck against the brick apartment building. My anxiety was high and I finally shouted at Calvin, "Get the fuck in because we are getting out of this bitch." With that, I scraped the truck against the brick building and we made the right turn finally. I was out of that situation and was now in a new situation with Calvin White. We were about to become best friends. Two weeks later, Calvin lost his apartment and moved above Breakshots with me in Oconomowoc. Breakshots is a bar in my hometown that caters to the local townie. At the time I moved there, the bar was on the decline as far as patronage goes. It was only filled with its die-hard regulars now. The guy who owned the bar was a little bit of a shady character in town, and would always want his rent in cash. Calvin was going to fit right in.

Calvin was yet another employee that didn't drive; if he stayed at a friend's house, I would have to go pick him up and drop him off wherever he needed to be. It was starting to be a pattern that The Junk Truck employees didn't drive. It's almost like if one of my employees had a car, they would just drive to apply for a different job. Shit, Calvin was in his early 20's and he didn't even hold a driver's permit yet. He just never took his driving test. On one occasion, the Junk Truck had a brake problem, and I asked Calvin, "Have you ever driven before?"

He was like, "Yes, but I don't have my license."

I shout out, "Whatever, just get in my Chevy and I will hop in the Junk Truck. You are going to follow me across town, so I can have a ride back." Calvin was so stunned that I would trust him to drive. No one trusted Calvin to do anything, so it was a big honor for him. I just kind of thought Calvin would be a good driver, so I let him drive my shit illegally. Through the years, I let him take my truck without a license to go get candy at the store. I really am fucking crazy!

Calvin White was a true blue friend to me... He put up with my bipolar mania with such ease. On one occasion I was driving the Junk Truck and I started beating the steering wheel so hard that I broke the horn. The horn in the green truck never worked again and eventually, the GMC emblem fell off the steering wheel almost suddenly resembling a NASCAR steering wheel. Nothing to it; just the wheel.

I broke both of the Junk Truck's horns by beating the steering wheel in a rage. Needless to say that Calvin was a tortured soul having to put up with the devil in disguise. Later, when I moved to a trailer park, Calvin left my power tools outside and I chased him down in broad daylight and screamed I was going to murder him. The worst part was his girlfriend Anna was watching in horror. Calvin had lived with me at my apartment above Breakshots and also in the trailer park. Above the bar, I came out of the shower naked and reenacted the opening scene in Terminator about wanting their clothes, boots, and motorcycle. We laughed so hard that night. Calvin truly understood my bipolar beauty. Our friendship blossomed from being young and wild and over the days it grew to winter and we expired into old bitter men. Rotten on the inside.

The Animal Hoarder

Real Junk Truck review

Name Withheld ★★★★★ 5/27/2011
Bay View, WI

Removal of old furniture and various
boxes of junk from a basement.
Prompt follow-up to e-mail inquiry
punctual. Did the job quickly, and
at the agreed price. Would
definitely use them again.

Calvin and I got a job on the outskirts of
Dousman, Wisconsin. It was a very big farm
property with endless acres of fields, outbuildings,
and a pretty big house. A middle-aged woman with
a butch haircut met us by the house on the hill.

Part of a junk removal estimate is walking
around to various different points of the property
and observing all the areas with junk that is going.
Then, you give an upfront, all-inclusive price for
the removal.

As we walked around the property, every
building had cages with animals living in them.
The outbuilding was converted into zoo-like
enclosures filled with ostriches, seals, and other
animals. Each enclosure was filled with animal
dung. It was so strange to see a farm turned into a
zoo. She covered the pool to house seals in what
would be a fancy mansion pool. Her enclosures
kind of reminded me of the jail cells on the Andy

Griffith Show. The jail cells were the stereotypical black iron bars you see in old television shows. I was expecting Barney Fife to turn the corner, but it was just a regular room or outbuilding converted into an animal jail. Like I said, there were animal droppings everywhere. She had us remove water-damaged furniture or boards or just random troughs for horses to feed from. While I was there, I wondered how she could afford this huge property and feed all the animals. I wondered what her high-paying profession was. We went into her barns and cleaned out dusty barn shit. I wanted to load the truck up fast because of my allergies. I am allergic to pet hair, so I was in a full-blown attack. We finished that day but she never called us again. Her job was too big for a truck service like mine; she was better off getting a dumpster and a couple goofballs.

Just the Tip

Real Junk Truck review

Name Withheld ★★★★★ 9/19/2012
Brown Deer, WI

Had the Junk Truck crew remove an
old pinball machine from our
basement and light cement drain
tiles and assorted cut log/tree
pieces from our backyard.

Utilizing a coupon from Angie's
List, I called The Junk Truck to
arrange a pick-up. I left a message
and my call was returned within a
short time. We arranged for a pick
up the next week. Travis, the owner,
and his helper arrived promptly at
the scheduled time. My husband
showed Travis the things we wanted
hauled away to see if the amount
would be covered using the coupon or
if there would be additional
charges. All was covered so we were
very pleased. We had dismantled the
pinball machine to make it easier to
carry but parts were still heavy.
The logs and other items were hauled
from our wooded backyard. Both
Travis and his helper were very
polite and professional. We would
definitely use them again.

A client called us during the week of my grandfather's wedding to my step-grandma. He sounded like a flamboyant older gentleman. He had a personality that was infectious, so I had joked with the client about how my grandpa is in a motorcycle gang and was having the trashiest biker wedding. My grandpa and his wife ended up having an eagle PowerPoint presentation at their ceremony. It was meant to show how 2 eagles come together. The client chuckled about how badass my grandpa is and said, "I have something growing in my garden that your biker grandpa would love; I will give it to you as a tip." He wanted the job midway through the week, so I said we would see him on Wednesday.

The client lived in a big white bungalow on the edge of the North Side of Milwaukee. It was a tall house with 3 stories with an urban garden in the backyard. He had a pile of junk in the backyard to haul off. He had a half load of construction debris, so Calvin and I loaded it up in a jiffy. The client told us about how he is divorced and just lives a party animal lifestyle now. As we shut the gates to the Junk Truck, he looked at us and said, "Now for the tip". He brought us back to a small garden of vegetables, and in between the tomatoes was a stinky marijuana plant. The female plant was just intermixed with a vegetable garden in some guy's backyard on the North Side!

I asked, "Your neighbors don't narc you out?"

He replied, "In this neighborhood, everyone keeps to themselves. People don't bother each other. No one minds if the plant is back here."

We awed at the sight of Mary Jane, but we wanted to experience her. The guy waved his hand and brought us down to his basement cellar. The client led us down a dingy basement with white wood paneling sectioning off different areas of the dungeon. He opened a canning closet and there were marijuana plants hanging upside down drying. He broke off a quarter of homegrown and threw it in a bag. The customer remarked, "Now, I have one rule, do not smoke while you drive the truck. Don't smoke this on the way home, boys!" We raced back home to my mom's, parked the truck, and drove to my apartment to smoke the homegrown.

The weed looked very homegrown and leafy, but it packed a punch! We sat in my apartment and smoked the whole quarter over a weekend. We listened to vinyl and sat back stoned; we couldn't stop laughing about how unorthodox that guy had been. Weed is more widely accepted today, but back in the 2000s, one plant could get you raided, lose your property, or in prison. I still think of that client to this day; I hope he has a field of dreams by this point.

When Nature Calls

Real Junk Truck review

Name Withheld ★★★★★ 6/8/2012
Hartford, WI

I had the junk truck remove an old
mattress, carpeting boxes and waste
out of my basement. Excellent job!
They were on time and efficient.

You are not a true junk man until you have
taken a plop in the back of your truck. Pissing in
the container only makes you a pledge to being a
journeyman. It is when you drop trou and really let
loose that reaches you to the top of the junk
removal summit. Until then, you are just an
amateur at best.

I did an estimate alone in Saint Francis.
Saint Francis is a suburb of Milwaukee. The
customer had all the junk waiting for me on the
driveway in the back towards the garage. I called
the client and shot the price of $250 for the half
truck. He agreed, so I started loading up the truck.
It was going to take a minute to sift through the
rubble of this construction debris. A quarter of the
way into the junk pick-up, I start having turd
flashes (these are hot flashes that you have dung
to drop). I had to poop so bad that I didn't have
time to finish the job and I didn't have time to

make it to the toilet at a gas station. I moved some more junk until I was crowning. I couldn't fucking take it anymore so I closed the back gates to the truck, pulled my pants down, and let a greasy turd slide out of my ass in the bed of the Junk Truck. I used some old clothes in the back to wipe up and powered through the rest of the job that Saturday morning.

On another occasion, Calvin ate some weird combination of Tornadoes from Speedway. His stomach was queasy as we passed 60th and Lincoln. Calvin demanded that I stop at this ghetto liquor store. He ran into the store and I didn't see him for 15 minutes. He came back a changed man.

He spoke of a tale of horror. The story was about Calvin being led into a backroom in the store that looked like the owner's family's living quarters. A Middle Eastern woman (owner's wife) was heating food up on a bunsen burner. Sleeping bags were strewn about the floor in this back room. Calvin relieved his newfound diarrhea, took off like a bat out of hell, and lived to tell me the tale. I am glad Calvin didn't end up in the Saw franchise.

Poop

Real Junk Truck review

Name Withheld ★★★★★ 9/13/2012
Brookfield, WI

I called on Wednesday and spoke to
Travis. By noon on Thursday all the
remodeling debris from the garage
and boxes, up to the size of a king-
size mattress, were removed and
loaded on the truck, very
conscientious and professional. I
will not hesitate to call again when
the next remodeling project is
complete.

The Junk Truck got a call to a senior living
facility. The job was on the second floor and was
your standard one-bedroom senior efficiency. It
was a one-room studio apartment of sorts. When
we stepped inside, the walls, carpet, and
countertops were white. I don't exactly remember
if the gentleman was dead, moved into the
Salvation Army, or was in hospice, but we were
informed he had a "pooping problem." *What the
fuck does that mean?* I was afraid of this job now.

First, we cleaned out the small living room
which had a couch and one of those octagon
tables your grandparents cherished in their
homestead. He had miscellaneous knick-knacks
piled up in the living room; we cleared out the

room in no time. Next, we moved on to his room. He had taken a shit in the bed. The white mattress had poop grime puddled in the middle of the mattress. Calvin was lifting up the bed with me to drag it out to the truck. As we lifted it, there was a pile of poop laying on the floor where the box spring and mattress were. Did this guy cover up a pile of poop by putting a bed over it? We held our breath, and Calvin screamed, "Nooooooo!"

Honestly, I probably cleaned the pile of shit up because I was so brainwashed into wanting to please the customer. I wanted our customers to believe that we were upstanding professionals and not really let them know we are druggie burnouts. The reason that I always wanted to go above and beyond was because I care about people; it meant a lot to me to help my customers. It was very fulfilling to solve a customer's headaches. It was almost an adrenaline rush to pick up the poop and see the customer impressed. It was like I was a junk god to people when I had poop in my hands; it meant that their problem was solved. We ended up finding a really big stamp collection at the job.

I ended up taking the stamp collection to this weird stamp business in the basement of a business building. I found him on Google, but I don't understand how you would know of this guy other than that. His stamp business was in a closet in the basement of this office complex. This flamboyant guy appeared in the closet, took one look at a page of stamps, and said, "Nah. I'm not interested. You should just use the stamps as free postage." He looked at like 2 pages of stamps and came to that conclusion. I ended up taking his advice, but I can't help but think of that piece of poop under the bed every time I lick one of those stamps and slap it on an envelope.

Stallis Sucker

Real Junk Truck review

Name Withheld ★★★★★ 7/31/2012
Jacksonville, FL

We are moving soon and we had lots
of junk/trash to haul out of here.
They were very professional and
nice. I was very happy with the
service! I would recommend them to
anyone. They offered a coupon that
provided great savings. It went very
well. They were prompt, courteous,
and professional.

West Allis, Wisconsin is a suburb of
Milwaukee that was established because of the
Allis Chalmers Factory. This has made life in West
Allis very blue-collar. Fast forward to now and
West Allis is filled with Juggalos, white trash, and
the elderly. Even though it is 2021, you will always
see a guy with no teeth in a 90's Packer Starter
jacket headed to a local Stallis tavern. The town
has been nicknamed the Dirty Stallis for its blue-
collar image.

One day, the phone rang and it was a
customer that had an uncle's property that
needed to be cleaned out. The guy thought it
would save him money if they had everything
outside waiting for us in the backyard. I told the
gentlemen, "We charge the same no matter what."

He agreed, but said, "I want to be there when you load up to make sure you are not overcharging me." Because of the schedule that day and his work schedule, I would not be able to let him supervise me loading my truck. We showed up early and loaded what I remember being construction debris. We had half the truck full, which I informed the guy, but he was insistent on seeing the load. I told him no matter what, it would still be a full load worth of material. We finished the job and went on to another job because the plan was to meet back later for this guy to pay me.

When I called him the guy said, "I can't meet because my car just broke down." I was starting to get weird vibes so I demanded that he meet. Calvin and I waited and suddenly this white trash guy showed up in a 90's sedan. In the front was what I'm guessing was his mother-in-law and his hideous wife. The guy was in a standard "I beat my wife" wife-beater. He also brought his son with him who was in a Packer's starter jacket.

Right away the guy is on the defense saying, "I don't want to pay because I never saw the size of the load." I said, "I wouldn't lie to you about the size of a load. My word is my bond."

He further insults me by saying, "This is just a shady way of doing business."

I'm thinking in my fucking head, "Are you serious, dude? You were fucking at work!" My response is, "JUST FUCKING PAY ME OR I WILL SUE YOU!"

"Calm down, man! This is no way to do business. You need to learn customer service." My blood is boiling and I know this guy is trying to get one over on me. I threaten to sue him and he finally agrees to pay. He keeps shooting his mouth off saying I'm a terrible businessman. The kicker is, as I'm finished running his credit card on my ancient credit card machine, the guy says, "You suck!"

His future carjacker of a son mimics the words, "You suck!"

Like father, like son! It felt so good to be told that I suck by a five-year-old boy! Nothing brightens your day more!

North Side Roaches

Real Junk Truck review

Name Withheld ★★★★★ 6/29/2012
Milwaukee, WI

Pick up and removal of electric
oven, elliptical trainer,
dehumidifier, stair-stepper, patio
umbrella, and Craftsman metal
workbench.

Bought the Angie's List coupon for
"junk removal" I contacted The Junk
Truck through the email address on
the coupon the evening I purchased
the coupon. I got an email response
saying they would contact me the
following day. They called the next
morning and I explained the items
that I wanted picked up and we
tentatively set up a time for that
afternoon.

The owner called around noon to ask
if it would be possible to
reschedule due to the heat. The
temperature was about 100 degrees
and there was a heat advisory in
effect. We rescheduled for Saturday
morning. The owner called Friday
morning to see if it would be
convenient to come Friday instead.
That was better for me.

They arrived on time, introduced
themselves and asked to see the
items to be removed. They worked
quickly and when they were done they
asked me to check to make sure they
got everything.

A slumlord who owned an apartment
complex on the North Side of Milwaukee lost his
units and the bank hired us to clean out a number
of units for them. The story was told to us that 75
percent of the tenants were being evicted
because they were a crackhead, a drug dealer, or
a hoodlum in general. Basically, the only people
who were left in this thirty-unit apartment complex
were four families.

We stepped in one of the units and Calvin
claimed to have seen bugs, so I told him I would
clean out this unit alone. I stepped inside and the
apartment was barren. There was a large, old
grandfather clock in the living room. Anything that
I picked up to haul out, like, 15 cockroaches would
run and scatter looking for darkness.

"Travis, don't panic. You got this." I moved
a box. Same thing. More cockroaches running for
the hills. I took the roach junk to the truck and saw
the children who live here. Even at my young age, I
felt for the kids who called this roach hotel home.
It made me realize how lucky I had it growing up
thirty miles west in suburban Oconomowoc. For a
moment, I gazed upon what life was really made of.
We were all human beings after all. In junk
removal, you have to see a lot of people living in

messed up situations. I had a very disturbing childhood, so I can always relate to people involved in the struggle. I understand what the kids have to go through with their living situations. Because of my messed up childhood, these types of situations made me develop a callus when being involved in their lives. Of course I was very gentle and nice to the kids, but it always reminded me about how some people are dealt hands that are out of their control. The only things I hope for are that those kids grew up to be productive members of society. It still never got easier to see people in such deep pain or suffering, so I had to develop a way for me to keep them in my heart but out of my mind.

I shook my head and headed inside for my next round of roach torture. I started to get anxious once inside again. I met up with Calvin who had been cleaning out a nearby unit. We went back to the truck where I had a complete tantrum like a fucking baby. Worse than a baby, actually. It was grey skies out and drizzling lightly on my face. A piece of garbage flew into the next complex over, but there was a fence separating me from it. I climbed the fence and my keyring with the truck keys broke off as I hoisted myself up to the top. The keys to my truck fell in overgrown, neglected grass.

I went into a fucking rage and panicked my way through a breakdown. Calvin was shaking his head, "Why did you climb after that garbage?"

I found almost all my keys except house keys. I was very lucky to be able to start the truck and drive back to Oconomowoc that day.

Lastly, we had to clean out the basement of the complex. It was like a fucking haunted house down there. It was all storage units made out of rickety old wood lined with fences. I thought Leatherface might have seen me as I cleaned out these cages. Each storage cage had multiple Swisher wrappers and Trojan Magnum condom wrappers littering each unit. The only thing I could think to myself was, *"Was someone being drugged and raped in these cages?"* My second thought was, *"At least they wore protection! I must be a fucking animal because I always have raw sex. What kind of animal am I?"*

Kitty Litter

Real Junk Truck review

Name Withheld ★★★★★ 7/1/2012
Oconomowoc, WI

Hauled away a truckload of old
fencing and yard waste. They were
prompt and courteous. When they
arrived, they introduced themselves
and explained the costs. I had an
"Angie's List Coupon, but it did not
cover everything I needed to be
done. I pointed out what needed to
be removed and they loaded it up on
the truck. They were very thorough
and did an awesome job! I have
absolutely no complaints and would
use them again any day. Moreover, I
would recommend them to friends and
family without hesitation.

    I got a call from a childhood friend who
moved away from Oconomowoc when we were
young. Shawn called the first number for junk
removal that he saw and it happened to be me. It
was funny that he called me thinking it was some
professional company, but it was just his
childhood friend Travis. He told me his mom was
moving out of Watertown. We booked them for the
second job that Saturday.

    Calvin left one weekend to be with his
vagina in Marengo, Illinois so I had Daron do a set

of jobs that day. Daron was a friend of a friend. He was a guy that just liked to play video games and smoke weed all day. He was a fast worker because he wanted to get back to his bud and video games. First, we went to a normal job that filled half the truck. The next one I suspected would be a truck, but because of the dump's prices, I needed to get a full load to unload the junk at the landfill. I went to the job with a half truck which always makes me sad because I should have wooed him as a customer, him being my childhood friend and all. The Junk Truck arrived at my friend's Mother's house.

The moment we stepped inside the house there was an extreme stench of cat piss. Shawn led us down to the basement where there were like 10 different litter boxes. Cat piss stained the white carpeting. Shawn pointed to black garbage bags that his mom had loaded up with soiled kitty litter, but never actually took upstairs and outside to the trash cans. The black bags were stinky and extremely heavy. Some of them broke apart as we pulled them upstairs.

Daron put on a mask as we loaded as much as we could in my truck; taking turns hauling bags of cat shit and piss upstairs. Cat hair was everywhere and really bothering my eyes and getting on my lips. We painfully filled the half truck and I sadly had to tell my childhood friend we couldn't finish today. I put him in a hard spot, but I was only one man and a truck, really. It kills me to this day that I couldn't help out a childhood friend.

The Riddler

Real Junk Truck review

When Calvin was out of town, I would use Daron, and when he was busy, I would use Daron's stepdad. We will call this character the Riddler. This was kind of a blue-collar guy that was a total stoner. He had long black hair and was close to or in his 50's. He had the build of someone who ate Mcdonald's every day. Everybody in town knew he was skeevy but he was a pretty nice guy for a con artist.

He was always scheming to get money, weed, or both. He had Jedi mind tricks that he would use to get scrap from you. He scrapped metal but claimed to need extra money so I gave him hours. This turned out to be a travesty.

The first job I took him to was for a really old client of mine. For this client, I cleared out these buildings that he owned in downtown Waukesha. Kevin and I had done that job. Now he wanted us to do a little junking for him but also move some things from storage to his house for him. The Riddler bitched the whole way because it started to downpour while we went from the storage unit to the guys.

The Riddler demanded, "You need to charge this guy for us doing those steps in the rain."

I was being mesmerized by his manipulation, so I said, "Okay. I will go tell them."

The Riddler started to demand more money from me for the day. He kept insisting that moving companies charge for the rain. Because I am such a pushover, I charged one of my all-time favorite customers a "rain charge." This is the perfect reason I don't own a junk removal company anymore. I could not handle these strong personalities like the Riddler. They would get one over on me for more money. Later in life, I worked for College Hunks and learned that there is no such thing as a "rain charge" for moving someone's stuff down steps in the rain.

The worst part was telling the customer about the rain charge. I could see in his eyes that he was very upset as rain pelted on the windows in their cottage. I still look back on this memory with a bitter taste.

The second memory I have of the Riddler is of a day that we picked up three fridges. On the way home the greasy, long-haired Riddler started to complain about the pay again. He would say, "You know, Travis, with only a few hours of work, this isn't really paying my bills." He then demanded that I give him the fridges for him to keep as scrap money.

Before I knew it, he was backing his truck up butt-to-butt with mine to load in the scrap. My mom came out and he quickly manipulated her into thinking him stealing business income from me was okay. I look back and laugh! What an asshole.

The last time I used this crazy maniac was when we got rid of a hot tub for a client in Oconomowoc. It was in Misty Meadows which is an older subdivision of the town. For some reason, he started treating me like I was an employee of The Junk Truck instead of the owner! He was suddenly wowing the customer and spewing recycling knowledge for the customer like, "You really need to recycle these transformers, Travis." Basically belittling me in front of my own customer.

He was putting on a show for the client and at one point the client said, "This guy is awesome. " *Little did that customer know, the Riddler was a grungy scumbag that smoked dirty resin out of pipes and grew crappy marijuana plants in his basement.* That is when it clicked that I needed to get away from this fucking John Wayne Gacy Pogo the Clown personality.

The Scam Artist

Real Junk Truck review

Name Withheld ★★★★★ 7/1/2012
Mequon, WI

We took advantage of this company's
promotion through Angie's List. Due
to their open schedule, they were
able to come within 2 days. We had
put everything out on the drive from
a garage and basement cleanout, and
they picked it all up and swept the
drive. The owner was friendly and
helpful. We would have them again.

They returned my initial call after
I purchased the service online. They
called to confirm the morning of the
pickup and were at our home for no
more than about 30 minutes because
we had everything out on the
driveway for them. They cleaned up
the area. While their truck may not
be real new, their service and
manner was professional and I'm
happy to support this business as it
grows.

The Junk Truck was really taking off at this
point; we were starting to have a high volume of
jobs. I got a call from a real estate agent from
Hartland about a property with fire damage near
Mequon. The agent stated he needed all the items
with fire damage to go, but he also booked it for a

Saturday. That meant that I probably couldn't haul away everything because the dumps closed early on Saturdays. The agent still booked with us, but there was already something off about him.

We drove to Mequon to find a dream home that had gone up in flames. The driveway was still stones which gave the indication that this house was still being built when it burned to the ground.

The agent was in his mini-SUV and there was a very old African American gentleman in overalls by a purple truck. In this story, we will call the old guy "Mr. Honest." I went to greet the agent and he swept me away to his truck and tried to make me sign a lien waiver.

This was my first red flag because you usually sign lien waivers after a payment is completed on a home that is for sale. My mom was a real estate agent and would always explain that the homeowners don't owe you anything if you sign one before receiving payment.

I told the agent that I would sign after being paid in full for the job. Next, the agent started to explain that they would pay me with the sale of the lot. This was my second red flag to run for the hills, but Mr. Customer Service wanted to take it up the ass from these goons.

I agreed to be paid out of the sale of the lot and Calvin, Daron, and I got to work hauling away burned junk.

The whole time, Mr. Honest, in overalls, kept throwing tantrums shouting, "She's the devil! She is a witch!" All my workers and I tried to keep to ourselves but were curious about the situation. The realtor told us the story while the black man took a breather.

Supposedly, Mr. Honest's wife and he were building their dream house in Mequon when it mysteriously burned down. They had been in a divorce battle during the time of the arson. The detectives ended up figuring out that the wife had hired a relative to burn the dream house to the ground, but when they went to talk to the relative, he had committed suicide. Now, there would never be a way to link the wife to the arson of the dream home in rural paradise.

The realtor and Mr. Honest really turned the heat up on us to get three trucks of junk loaded that day. I was starting to feel the forces of anxiety running a business because of all the clients freaking out on us to clear out big junk piles. People expected us to work a miracle for them. This is one of the times in the business that I should have expanded because I ended up having to cancel on a client for the second week in a row. This was due to the fact that the realtor and Mr. Honest coerced me into the last load of black soot junk for the day.

We hauled off our last load and expected the sale of the lot to pay for our troubles, but fate, I mean, Cunt Rag, would intervene. "Cunt Rag" is going to refer to Mr. Honest's wife. She doesn't deserve a human being's name in this story.

So one day, I was stoned out of my mind at my apartment in Oconomowoc and I got a call from a weird number. I answered and immediately a woman started screaming at me in such a cartoonish way that I honestly considered it a prank call.

She stated that her name is Cunt Rag, wife of Mr. Honest, and that we hauled away all her possessions from the house. I laughed out loud and told her, "That's impossible! All of your possessions were burned to black soot!"

This scorned Cunt Rag fired back in a wicked tone, "You stole my $10,000 piano!"

Again, in shock, I said, "Your piano has serious fire damage to the point of not being keepable or playable."

Cunt Rag started screaming and threatening to sue me over all her items that were scorched in the fire she paid someone to set. She hung up, and I laughed a little because of how out of left field that was.

That was until the Waukesha Sheriff went to my parent's house looking to serve me papers. I drove down to the Waukesha County Courthouse. I waited for the cop on the case to hand me paperwork. He came out with documents that had

me as a defendant and Cunt Rag as the plaintiff.
THE FUCKING CUNT RAG WAS SUING ME FOR
$10,000 FOR HER BURNT JUNK!

I literally wigged out in front of the officer
and asked him, "How this is even fucking real?"
That day I realized that the American Dream is
horse shit. I was being sued by a known scam
artist/criminal, and there was nothing I could do to
get out of it.

I got home to my apartment and got a call
from Cunt Rag's husband. He apologized and
said, "Travis, this woman is the devil!" The
husband claimed that after their divorce, Cunt
Rag had sued him over 13 different times. Mr.
Honest also claimed that every company Cunt
Rag comes in contact with, she ends up taking to
court because she refuses to work.

Cunt Rag forced me against my will to hire
a really expensive attorney that I didn't have
money for, all because I couldn't prove that her
stuff had fire damage. Cunt Rag claimed the
piano was in pristine shape, but in reality, it was
burned and covered in ashes. I just wanted to
fucking scream because all I was doing was trying
to make a living for a guy with severe bipolar
disorder.

The real estate agent, me, and her
husband all got sued in court over burnt rubbish. I
spent $1,500 on a lawyer only for a judge to
research Cunt Rag's court history. Right away, he

recognized that she was a career scam artist. She had sued over 30 companies which were all visible through public records. It was kind of cool to have my lawyer go on my behalf and see court documents that said so and so attorney was there "on behalf of Mr. Geier."

You are probably wondering how Mr. Honest got his name? Well. . . even all through this, Mr. Honest paid all the money for the three loads that were taken out of the property. I will never forget how his word was his bond. He had the Devil breathing down his neck, yet he still paid me for getting thrown into this mess. I stayed in touch with Mr. Honest all through our trial. The last time we spoke was when my case got thrown out. We wished each other well.

Broken Dreams

Real Junk Truck review

Name Withheld ★★★★★ 10/3/2012
Menomonee Falls, WI

They hauled away an old pool liner
and the remains of a dismantled
wooden playground set. As well as a
couple of very heavy garbage bags.
The junk was all in our backyard and
they carried it all to the front
where their truck was.

We called in the morning and they
were at our house in a few hours.
They were very professional and
courteous and explained all the
costs and procedures up front. They
packed the truck in such a way that
we only had to pay for ¼ truckload-
they could have just tossed it in
and charged for half. Very impressed
and would highly recommend.

In 2020, I did a job with Junk King where I
was reminded of how awkward it is when we have
to remove junk in a room where someone is
sleeping. We went to this crackhead's house,
gave them a quote, and we started moving the
junk out to the truck. They had a huge mattress in
the basement that didn't go; which I was very
relieved about. On my coworker and I's trip down
to the basement for a second helping, we notice a
guy laying in bed and are startled that we didn't

notice him in his jammies trying to sleep. They did have a futon frame that needed to be brought upstairs, and we were both terrified we might have to tell this sleepy head he might need to move. We got the frame out while he stared at us. As the frame went up the stairs, it had me thinking of another awkward job with The Junk Truck many years ago.

The Junk Truck got a job for a couple of televisions in the hood. We get anally penetrated each time we have to pick up TVs because of the electronic disposal cost. They are not even worth picking up, but a job is a job, so we head to this run-down house on the North Side of Milwaukee.

An attractive African-American woman answered the door and led us up a winding staircase of an old Polish house. We head to an attic apartment, and she brings me and Calvin in a room with a very muscular African-American man laying naked with just a sheet around his cut body. Calvin and I tiptoed by his bed to look at the smashed flatscreens. So I whispered to her that it would cost 79 dollars for this pickup.

She gave a very strange look, and shot back, "Y'all don't pay me for my TVs?"

Calvin and I looked very strange at each other because we knew that it cost an arm and a leg to dispose of the flat screens. I explained that we have to pay to get rid of them; the customer didn't seem to care. She just wanted us out the second that we couldn't fulfill her request. I now felt trapped because we were doing this estimate with a naked guy, covered in a sheet, and he was tossing and turning like he wasn't getting a good rest. We quickly left the apartment and headed back to my green junk truck without the flatscreens. We headed back to Oconomowoc.

Most Expensive Shit

Real Junk Truck review

Name Withheld ★★★★★ 3/19/2011

I was impressed with how hard these guys worked and how nice they were. I'm grateful to have my basement back again. Thanks, Junk Truck

I get asked all the time, "What is the most expensive junk anyone has given you?" The answer is simple: money! Customers have literally been too lazy to cash coins in, so they would just hand me real money.

The first time I was handed coins was by a Harley-Davidson motorcycle engineer. He wanted to have his uncle's house cleaned out. His uncle had passed away and was somewhat of what I would call a tool hoarder. The deceased uncle was a handyman and had tools all over his Bayview home. The engineer had me come take 2 loads a weekend until the house was cleared out.

All of the uncle's stuff was old, dusty, and heavy. The last weekend we were finishing up the cleanout, it was a brutal job with all the heaviest items left. I started to get in a bad mood at the end.

We were finally done when the customer said, "I have something really heavy upstairs, and if you can haul it, it's yours." I was fucking annoyed because I wanted to stop lifting heavy, old shit. I was surprised as he brought us up the stairs to find 2 glass carboys filled with ancient pennies. My jaw fucking dropped as I stared at the copper goldmine. We barely could move them to my truck, and we could barely get the money in the back of the bed. I ended up selling some of the old pennies and cashing in the rest. I ended up making an extra $450 from the pennies.

The next time I got money was from a job at a house located in a private golf course/country club. This rich couple was getting rid of a pile of junk and construction debris in their basement. They brought me down and said, "Everything in the middle of the room is to go!"

As I took a box up, I noticed some coins were in 2 orange pill jars. I put them in the truck and finished hauling the debris out of the basement. I took the coins home and called my uncle whose dad is a coin collector.

My uncle's dad wanted me to bring them to his house, so I did. His dad got that weird magnifying glasses headset on and looked at the coins. They were Benjamin Franklin coins and he said they were mostly made of silver. He kept ooh-ing and ahh-ing at the coins. He finally informed me he would be buying the coins from me. He wrote me a check that read, "$870.00" I could not believe it! It still amazes me to this day when people throw out real money or real jewelry. One man's trash is another man's treasure!

Negligence

The truck was from 1986, so it loved to do this act of kindness where it would break down a lot. It would never break down empty. The truck would always not start after we had loaded the truck to the brim with junk. The vehicle being such a piece of shit mechanically gave it true meaning to the words, "Junk Truck."

One junk job took us to a customer's house who had somewhere to be that Saturday. I backed the truck up to his garage where his car was stowed away. We loaded his junk up, collected payment, and hopped in the truck. I turned the ignition, and nothing happened....

I was so embarrassed; we had to go knock on the door and break the news that he wasn't going anywhere because we needed a tow truck. We had to wait over 50 minutes for the right size tow truck to be able to tow the truck that was now full of 1 ton of trash inside. The customer was cool, calm, and collected while we waited for the tow truck to arrive. Finally, the rig arrived to tow away my embarrassment. The tow truck driver just calmly got the truck on the rig and we left the scene of embarrassment.

The next dumb shit I did was that I did a trade with Fox Music in Watertown. I was to remove a huge amount of these huge sheets of glass. The glass was the size of a sheet of drywall.

Regularly, I rode my bicycle from my apartment in Oconomowoc to Fox Music in Watertown, so I had gotten to know the owner pretty well. The owner lived just down the street from the music shop, and he lived next to his dad. His dad had these sliding door size panes of glass. All the glass was stacked up behind the house.

Junk removal estimates can be hard because every job is different, so it's hard to know what you're getting into. This time, I was just being an idiot and wanted to do the job of glass sheets for just a measly $150 in trade of vinyl to be ordered at Fox Music. I had no idea what moving glass would be like. I was in for a real treat because every pane of glass was ungodly heavy.

Calvin and I drove out with the Junk Truck to go get the glass about a week later. Calvin took one look at the backyard with about 50 or 60 sheets of sliding door size glass. I watched Calvin's eyes bulge out like a Looney Tunes Character. He said, "You bid this for $150 worth of records? Travis! This is going to be so dangerous. The glass is taller than us!"

I started to get anxious about what Calvin had to say next. He said, "I don't know if your truck can carry this much glass. You will break your springs." I was suddenly having concrete flashbacks to the old days with Jesus and the concrete we broke up.

Perspiration was setting in as I dug out the dolly from the back of the truck. We would have to try to set the humongous glass panes on the dolly upright without breaking the glass and possibly being cut in half through our torso. I didn't realize how dangerous the glass was going to be. My stupidity never took into account that these sheets of glass, as big as us, could break and gravely puncture us.

The next problem was how we had to carry the glass on the dolly. It had to be stood upright, but the glass was so heavy you had to steady it with something. Both my hands were full with the dolly, so I had to put the glass on my chin kind of. This was a great moving practice if you wanted to have your head decapitated.

We would over-stack the dolly with too much glass, I would struggle to chin it over to the truck, and then we would almost die by guillotine trying to load them sideways on the back of the truck. The truck had no ramp or lift to bring the sheets of death up to the bed of the Junk Truck. This made it totally unsafe to stack the glass as the glass pile became higher. Let alone that I had the truck filled with another job to save money on dumping a load.

As we loaded the last sheets, I was having a panic attack about several different scenarios. *What if we lose a limb from the glass falling on us? What if the truck won't drive because the glass is too heavy? What if I slit my throat on this glass trying to carry too many sheets of glass?* These were questions that ran through my mind, but I was too deep in this junk move now.

The glass was so heavy that we struggled to walk with the sheets on that dolly. It felt like I was moving pyramid stones for the rock and roll gods. The one hundred and fifty dollar credit that I got for the records wasn't worth it! Fuck, was this a learning a lesson! I underbid the guy so bad! We eventually got all the glass loaded and the truck was slightly leaning to the left.

I closed the gates to the back and told the guy I would be in next week to order my records, and I got in the cab to pray that my truck would pull the load of glass. I started and the truck pulled away like a champ! It wasn't until months later when the Junk Truck broke down on the side of the highway, that a tow driver yelled at me because I had broken the leaf springs on my truck, and was still pulling loads with it. Leaf springs provide suspension for big loads on your truck. My truck was lopsided now from the break. It was bad. I felt so stupid because I had broken my truck for music records, but at least I had Times of Grace, GG Allin, and Obituary on vinyl now!

Spit

One moment stands out in my mind as the moment that I stopped giving a shit about the business. Up to this point, I was doing a very professional job in front of customers. We had withstood the test of time by this point; we had lasted more than five years in business. We had survived the scam artist, but my gears were starting to grind slower as we went along. I prided myself on having amazing customer service, but I was starting to wear my customers' demands on my sleeves.

Mokè and I had a small job in Whitefish Bay on a Saturday. We met with a short, Asian man that showed us different piles around his yard. It was a smaller job, so this seemed like it would be another success. I started to haul some wood to the truck from the backyard. The man was watching us intently as we hauled the wood from the backyard. I liked to talk to my customers to make them feel like I was personable, but this time was different. I was in a manic episode without realizing it. In the recent weeks, I had started to gradually smoke more and more weed. I had over thirty thousand in my business account, but I was rapidly pulling out money to feed my addictions. My bank account was starting to shrink as it went up in smoke.

I was starting to make mistakes during jobs that made me look really bad to my customers. It was at this customer's house that I felt a shift in my life that I would never recover from. While talking to the short, Asian man, I spit on his grass in his backyard. Once the spit left my mouth and hit the ground, I was never going to be the same.

The man looked at the ground and said, "Travis, that is very disrespectful that you would spit on the ground in front of me."

I was uneasy at this point and replied, "I am so sorry sir!"

He looked puzzled for a while then asked, "Travis, were you in the military?"

I said, "No, I never was in the service."

The man looked more puzzled than before and said, "I could understand if you spit because you were in the service in your younger years. Most servicemen like to chew tobacco."

I didn't know how to respond to that statement, so I just nervously shrugged it off. I remember that the man then handed us a Super Nintendo that was still in the original box. I stared at the box thinking to myself that I was slipping in my life. I had weirded out this customer because my life was becoming bizarre in itself. I wanted to get the job over with because I had screwed up. Looking back, I realized that this was the moment of the point of no return. Just a simple wad of spit lay on the green grass; symbolizing what was to come. That wad of spit referenced that I wasn't the same Travis that would bend over backwards for his clients. That spit represented a change in the way that I would look at the week's workload. I left that day knowing that gentlemen would never call me back for another job. My bipolar mania was setting in on me and I would never recover from it until a decade later...

Grandpa, Take the Wheel

Real Junk Truck review

Name Withheld ★★★★★ 7/24/2012
Brookfield, WI

Hauled junk from the basement and other areas of the house including many reams of old papers. They were very hard working and took extra stuff that wasn't in the original agreement. I feel that I definitely got my money's worth from this company. It was a pleasure working with you.

By this point in The Junk Truck, I was just going through the motions of the junk jobs. It's hard when every job you get is a loved one whose parents died, and they live in Arizona and are in a time crunch for this cleanout. I was starting to slip with paying bills, answering phones, and getting up early. My mom called me to inform me that I had been driving the Junk Truck for a few days with no driver's license. She had already called my grandpa to drive the truck for a few days. Remember, my grandpa is in a biker gang and is a very interesting character to be around, so Calvin loved how blunt my grandfather could be.

My grandpa filled in as the driver for a week straight until my license was reinstated. My grandpa used to be a garbage man with a commercial run. He worked for Laidlaw Sanitation. In the '80s my grandpa was the guy that dumped the garbage behind restaurants. He said the worst can to dump was that of a Chinese restaurant. The sweet sauces would create maggots in the dumpster. Yummy!

After driving for a week, he was reminded about how much of pigs that garbage men are. Calvin and I would spend all our drive time looking at the nastiest, hardcore porno magazines. My grandpa told a story about a time that he was dumping a load of garbage at the landfill. Someone spotted porn and the landfill completely shut down until the holy grail of filth was saved from sudden death.

My grandpa said, "You guys are fucking nasty!" He also urged me to get my driving permit back so I can resume jobs without him. He was no spring chicken after all. I couldn't have a senior citizen at every job; especially a crazy old biker.

Up the Wall

Real Junk Truck Review

Name Withheld ★★★★★ 2/20/2012
Wauwatosa, WI

Removed accumulated stuff from our
basement. Good experience.

I got my license back at this point; it felt
good to hit the pavement again. A job was booked
on the outskirts of the North Side of Milwaukee.
The great part was that the job was 10 minutes
from the dump. Calvin and I drove right past the
location of the job because it didn't look like
anything was there. It looked like just a little patch
of brush by the freeway. We rammed the Junk
Truck up its hill and came upon what looked like a
dilapidated old one-room schoolhouse.

This lady greeted us and led us inside the
moldy schoolhouse. Once inside, the inside
looked like we were outside. The interior was
covered in wet wood and moss on the wall. The
ground had leaves scattered everywhere like we
were at a park. The lady just wanted the inside
cleaned out and planned to sell this off the beaten
path property as is.

The inside looked like a rotten, moldy
homestead. As we picked up a dresser, a squirrel
jumped out and ran up the moldy wall! Calvin was

like, "Fuck this, dude! We got things crawling up the wall and shit."

Calvin, again, was a trooper and kept going and yet again, something was moving around in there. Would we end up like Steve Irwin, get bit or stung and blubber over in death? I probably should have called off the job, but the job was an impossible job to finish. A lot of the furniture inside was turning to dirt, so we cleared out the big items and left the rest. The lady seemed very pleased that we did a good job and didn't contract rabies.

Bug Bomb

Real Junk Truck review

Name Withheld ★★★★★ 7/10/2012
Muskego, WI

They removed some old metal
shelving, a lawn mower, basketball
hoop, etc. They were very quick.
They actually even cleaned out the
grill that they hauled away.

I had just bought a mobile home in the
Milwaukee area. Sometimes I wish that I would
have stayed above Breakshots because I could
have never imagined what was in store for me in
Milwaukee.…. The city was a nice change, but I was
soon reminded of the hustle and bustle of city life.
It was just supposed to be an estimate…
one fucking estimate… Calvin was living in the
trailer with me during this time, so we took my white
Chevy Colorado to an estimate on the South Side
of Milwaukee. The South Side is filled with
prostitution and drugs. A lot of the properties are
infected with hoarding.

This house was no different. We arrived in
front of a brick building. The bricks were dark like
a black turd of the dying. It was eerie, too,
because there were no lights inside. Some hotshot
Latino landlord let us in. He made sure to let us
know it would just be an estimate and he had
other companies bidding.

Calvin and I walked around yet another hoarding situation. The house had sleeping bags all strewn about like they had multiple people just crashing. It was typical with the basement being completely packed with useless junk. The house was very dirty. I told the landlord it would be multiple truckloads, and we got back inside my truck. Calvin was already in a bad mood because of some bullshit I probably pulled.

We stopped at a stoplight, and Calvin started freaking out! He yelled, "We have fleas now!" We both started slapping ourselves as I noticed little black bugs jumping around us.

We were driving by this point and looked like cartoon characters getting in a fighting cloud. Calvin was screaming, "That job gave us fleas, dude!" He was so fucking mad at me. I called my mom freaking out and she told us to head to Menard's to get a bug bomb.

Calvin was really mad and awkward as we walked the aisles of this big home improvement store with fleas. We selected the trusted name of Off!, and we went to my truck, and bombed the truck right there in the parking lot. We stood together and sort of laughed, but Calvin was still mad at me for giving him fleas.

We had to wait a hot minute before we could open the truck, roll the windows down, and leave for the trailer.

We ended up stripping down on my porch in our undies to avoid bringing the fleas in my trailer, but to no avail, the trailer had fleas until the day I sold it. Fuck... We even tried to bug bomb the trailer on two different occasions. Pesky fuckers...

Donaldson Drive

Real Junk Truck review

Name Withheld ★★★★★ 10/9/2012
Brookfield, WI

They picked up various items that I
no longer wanted from the basement,
upstairs, garage, and yard. They
removed a sleeper sofa from the
basement, as well as a dresser, a
desk, two chairs, and a pallet. They
carried out an old TV from a
bedroom, then various items from the
garage and the yard.

They arrived on time and got to work
right away after I showed them the
items that I wanted them to take.
They were two men and they worked
very methodically and quickly. After
they finished they asked me to make
sure they had gotten everything. I
was very impressed with their work.

We did a cleanout for one of the
professional organizers from the A&E show
Hoarders. The little man's name is Braiden
Howard and he is a little bald munchkin. Braiden's
favorite thing to do to a hoarder was to steal
something of value from them, and then tell the
family that it had to go. Braiden would then take
the item home and hawk it on eBay. I know this
because Calvin was family friends with Braiden

Howard and his pathetic Class Action Organizing business.

We started to meet Braiden at a job every weekend in Waukesha. It was an old woman that was a hoarder for 30 years. Braiden would have me park my truck on the side and then we would usually have some talk about, "My client needs a break on the cost of truckloads". Haha, but the fat pig had no problem charging the old lady his rate of $50 an hour!

Anyway, this lady's house was just filled with filth. All of her house was filled with moldy junk with cat piss and shit on it. I felt bad because Braiden was taking these people for a ride, but I just kept my mouth shut and hauled away the rubbish. Braiden would stand with this old woman as he convinced the old lady's family she was crazy, so he could get his nubs on her antiques!

One day on Donaldson Drive, it really stood out where I knew that hoarding was a very sad mental illness. Braiden came up to us and said, "The old woman won't get rid of a chair. So I will stall her and you tiptoe the chair out from behind her back."

When we got the cue, we walked like cartoon characters trying not to wake up the old monster. The chair was covered in mouse poop, pee, and had a broken spring coming out of the cushion for some kind of sick anal penetration.

The old hoarder turned around and saw us mid-move with the chair. She shrieked, "No! I need that chair!"

Braiden replied, "There is mouse poop on it; I can't let you have this chair because I could lose my professional organizing license. Plus, there is a spring sticking out."

The hoarder screamed, "But I can fix it!" Braiden waved us forward to throw the chair in the truck.

Calvin and I started to move this mouse shit-covered chair, when the hoarder started shouting "No! NO! NO!"

We went up the back of the hill, to the side of the house, and threw the chair in the back. Thinking about the hoarder now, in my thirties, I can understand her wanting to hold her possessions close. The world can be a bitter place, and it feels good to have stuff to come home to.

The Dispute

Real Junk Truck review

Name Withheld ★★★★★ 6/28/2012
Milwaukee, WI

Service was not provided because I did not meet the terms and conditions. Money was refunded.

Service provided was courteous. He explained why I did not meet the terms and conditions for his service. I understood based on his explanations. He was very professional and congenial. He offered me a refund and I accepted.

A representative in marketing is someone who helps you with your marketing strategy. Even in the 2010's the internet had become so confusing with social media, websites, and search engines that it is helpful to have someone helping you with the back end of your marketing. Pete Schlosser was my mentor and representative that helped me get the Junk Truck off the ground. I met him by putting fliers in his neighborhood. He helped me scale the business's revenue. He had switched positions and could not be my representative at AT&T anymore. I was set up with this new representative that lived around Lake Country. We agreed to meet her at a coffee shop in nearby Delafield.

The day of the meeting, my mom and I went to meet the rep in Delafield. My mom pulled in with her Acura MDX, and another car almost hit us. They didn't try stopping even though we pulled in before they raced to basically smash into us. We got out of the SUV and the car that almost intentionally hit us stopped. They were waiting for us; I could see two women in their 20's inside and they were pointing at my mom and mouthing the words, "You are a fucking whore."

I am not prejudiced against who needs an ass beating. I was going to beat the fucking shit out of this cunt-rag who called my mom a whore. I walked up and started bashing my fist against her window to break it. I was going to break her window and drag her out of the car to apologize to my mom. The weak pig cunt started calling the cops, so we went inside to meet our rep about our new marketing strategy. The cops showed up in the coffee shop and just pulled me and my mom by the two squad cars.

The cops asked for my side of the story, but I basically had suffered amnesia the moment I saw the red and blue. I just kept denying everything. The police kept using their entrapment techniques to make me and my mom confess, but Geiers don't go out like that. We were let off and headed into the meeting to meet my new very quirky sales rep.

The sales rep was a heavyset woman in her 50's; she claimed to have worked for the marketing aspect of AT&T for over a decade, but

129

the more she talked about Google and SEOs, we realized that she was some dumb old woman that didn't know jack shit! My mom and I knew more about Google marketing than what was in her absent mind. My mom and I were both shaken from the confrontation with the police, so it was hard to hear this rep blabber about shit she knew nothing about. I told my lawyer friend and he said that his law office was assigned to this particular person at one point. He also agreed that she didn't know fuck about advertising. I ended up literally hating this rep so much that I pulled my AT&T advertising. No one uses the Yellow Pages anymore anyway.

Putrid

Real Junk Truck review

Name Withheld ★★★★★ 9/29/2012
Milwaukee, WI

Great company! These guys really
worked hard. They were timely and
professional. They completely
removed every item and hauled it
away to the dump, Goodwill, and
other donation centers. Excellent!
This was a really big job and they
completed it without complaint or
extra fees.

Our nastiest job that comes to mind was in
one of the richest areas of Wisconsin. The setting
was the suburbs in a town called Burlington. The
house was a pretty good size, had a red and gray
color scheme, and was definitely built by a
homebuilder in the modern era of the pre-
recession boom.

We received a call from a subcontractor
from Illinois that was trying to get the house on the
market because the house was in foreclosure. The
guy on the other end of the phone wanted a total
trash out meaning everything was to go in the
home.

We arrived at the house with junk already
in the back of the truck for some stupid reason.
Calvin tried to organize the back of the truck to fit

131

more Junk without much success; meanwhile, I went to the lockbox to retrieve the key.

We stepped inside to a deep smell of rotting food. The floors of this nice modern house have puddles of green slime stuck to them. The house is a big hoarding situation.

That fucking smell though was so strong that we ended up going to grab stuff from the basement that was packed full.

We went into the garage to find something big to fill the truck up with to get out of there. We saw a huge, old white chest freezer. We both agreed to grab it, but for some reason, I needed to see what was inside the chest. Was it a human corpse?

I opened the top of the freezer and literally one hundred flies came buzzing out of the fucking freezer. That number is not some exaggeration from an author; one hundred files came out of the motherfucker.

Calvin and I ran in horror like we were in an Alfred Hitchcock film. We regrouped by the truck. *What did we just go through?* I called the client and told him this might be out of our wheelhouse.

The guy got mad and said, "I thought you were a full-service junk removal business?" with a snarky attitude. I informed him that this job was at a biohazard level. He bitched and told me to keep going. We bit the bullet and ventured back inside the Hell house.

We thought to start in the basement next to grab whatever we could to fill the truck. There were blankets just covering the basement stairs. They almost looked like giant Anacondas waiting to carry me down and devour me. We pulled on the blankets like a cartoon robber getting his loot bag cut at the bottom, and the blankets came up.

We noticed right away that the blankets were covered in human feces. Disgusted, we quickly got the blankets out of the house and went downstairs for more.

Next, we brought blankets up and we found human feces on the quilts. We realized that they had kids who would soil the bed. Instead of washing the sheets and blankets like normal parents, they would just buy a new set of sheets and blankets and throw the soiled linens down the basement stairs for later. Well… Later never came for these parents because there was a mountain of shit sheets!

I called it right there! I called the client and informed him this was pure biohazard and to call a hazmat team. This was human waste. This Illinois contractor was so fucking pissed off, but a week later my mom got a call from him. He apologized for questioning our integrity as a junk outfit because the hazmat team told him we absolutely made the right call pulling out of that job.

Sometimes when I'm right, I'm right. Victory is mine!

Hot Tub Terrorist

Real Junk Truck Review

Name Withheld ★★★★★ 7/10/2012
Wales, WI

I called Junk Truck to remove a
large old hot tub. I got a quote
over the phone for 2 prices
depending on size. They came out
promptly on the scheduled day, which
was within a day or two of the first
call. They confirmed the price on
arrival. They sawed the unit into
quarters there on the deck and
loaded it into the truck. They did
an excellent job of cleaning up.
This entire job was handled over the
phone and we did not have to be
there for the work, which made it
very convenient. We also used the
Junk Truck coupon from Angie's List
which is figured in the price. That
was a half coupon up to the max
value of $158 I paid $79 online for
the coupon and saved $79 off the
quoted $358 price. I paid the
balance of $227 to Junk Truck on
completion. I am providing these
details only because there was some
confusion with Junk Truck on how the
coupon worked. Sometime later they
also sent a bill for the work that
had already been fully paid. I am
happy to say that we worked it out

over the phone easily and to my satisfaction. I gave them a B on professionalism only for the confusion. The work was great and I would use them again.

By this time, I was burned out doing junk removal. All I wanted to do was get high to forget about having to follow through with these jobs. I got an add-on call to estimate a hot tub in Oconomowoc. I now lived in West Allis, which was 30 miles from Oconomowoc, so I wasn't right in town anymore. We showed up at a nice house in the city; I grabbed my Junk Truck clipboard and walked around with the guy. We laughed and joked about living in Oconomowoc. We even had a chuckle about what it was going to take to cut up the hot tub to haul it off. The estimate ended up being what I would consider a model estimate. If I were to make a training video, this estimate would have been the opening scene.

What is a model estimate you ask? It would start with no garbage falling out of my truck the moment that I stepped out of the Junk Truck. Next, I wouldn't wobble to the door in a burned-out, "I was stoned all night" kind of way. Next, I would knock at the door with my clipboard with the official Junk Truck pricing. Lastly, I would walk through the house with my potential client just spewing bullshit that made me look good. I would say something in the vein of, "Every year, the world consumes so many water bottles that the bottles could circle around the Earth's atmosphere 26 times." These facts that I looked up online made the potential customer think, "This guy knows his stuff!" We would usually get hired after a model estimate and we would usually do a good job for them.

I got back in the Junk Truck and Calvin and I took off for Milwaukee which sadly was home now. Halfway to Milwaukee, I realized that I left my clipboard back at the customer's house. Fuck! I wanted to get high so fucking bad that I blew up in a fucking road rage!

I started screaming and beating the fuck out of the steering wheel. Calvin was in the passenger seat frozen with fear. I was having a nervous breakdown because we would now have to drive 50 more minutes. I was screaming so violently that I was shaking the Junk Truck.

After my psychotic break, I looked down at my smartphone and saw that I had butt-dialed the client during my bipolar breakdown!

Now, I was the one who was scared! We made it back to the hot tub property and I ran to the door, knocked, and waited. There was no answer, but I could hear rumblings inside. I knocked again because I wasn't leaving without my Junk Truck clipboard. The clipboard had a laminated price list that a graphic designer laid out for me; I couldn't leave it behind! There were graphs of the truck to show sizes. I needed it back!

His son answered the door with a spooked look on his face like he had seen a ghost. His dad beelined it on the side of the house with the clipboard in hand. The dad had a very uneasy vibe like he was handing Jeffrey Dahmer his drill back.

I said, "Thank you!" and I never heard from him again. I somehow can still live with myself after thinking about that moment in my life. My bipolar can be super embarrassing if it is not in check.

The Great Piano Disaster

Real Junk Truck review

Name Withheld ★★★★★ 7/30/2012
Brookfield, WI

We had a phone conversation before
they arrived, during which the owner
stated he would have to see the
piano before determining the actual
cost to haul away. He did give us a
range of what it would cost. When he
arrived and took one look at it, he
informed us it would be at the
lowest cost range he had provided.
These guys were punctual, polite,
and--best of all--they try to find a
use for some of the stuff they haul
away. We would definitely use them
again!

Two memories really haunt me deeply to
this day. One took place on a piano job. I used my
lunatic grandpa for piano removal because he
used to be a mover for Allied Van Lines in the
1970s. He usually would MacGyver boards under
the piano somehow. Magically, the pianos would
get loaded up even though they were so heavy.

On this occasion, I woke up late in my
trailer with a crazy panic attack. I was late! I had to
go pick Calvin up from the East Side from a group
of friends, who hated me at the time because I had

gone ballistic on one of them in a bipolar episode. I sat in shame in my truck and Calvin eventually appeared out of the party house.

We drove 15 minutes to Brookfield to a nice upper-middle-class house. I saw my grandpa's truck parked out front. Fuck! The crazy man was already in the basement where the piano was! We knocked. A very tense-looking man answered the door and told us. "He is downstairs!"

I go downstairs with Calvin to see my grandpa sawing a piano key off in a beautiful basement with brand new expensive tile. I was sure we would damage the floor and we fucking did! My grandpa looked crazy with his safety glasses on as he sawed away. In between cuts, he made remarks like, "Why are you late to your own job, Travis?"

The answer came to my mind. The reason was because I was letting weed consume me!

We could not bring that piano up the stairs! There was no fucking way! My grandpa just kept sawing away at the fucker. Calvin noticed my vintage White Zombie shirt. He told me, "That shirt is old school, Travis! So rad!" I nervously agreed. The problem was that we kept moving the piano on the tile creating these black marks that did come off with scrubbing. I was horrified to be trapped in this guy's basement with this problem. My grandpa, Calvin, and I made several attempts to drag the sawed piano to the basement steps, but when it came time to actually walk upstairs with the piano, it was just unrealistic.

I ended up telling the customer that we couldn't get it upstairs. The dude had a sinister look in his eyes. He let us out of his house without saying a word. For the next few months, he called my mom and harassed her. A business is a weird force because even when you aren't ready to do jobs, you fucking have to anyway.

Cougar

Real Junk Truck review

Name Withheld ★★★★★ 10/8/2012
Milwaukee, WI

They arrived promptly. They took a
dining room table, 5 chairs, and an
old console radio. When I mentioned
that I had the extra leaves in the
basement, they took them, too. They
were very professional and handled
all the furniture well. Took about
20 minutes.
As above. Without a doubt, I would
hire them again.

I always got asked a ton if I ever had sex
with any of my clients. Everyone knows that old
porn trope about the serviceman coming to fix the
pipes. The answer is I did come close, but my
conscience came in at the final hour.

This woman called and her last parent had
died. Her sister was moving into the house
because she was the deadbeat of the family. It
happened to be in my hometown of Oconomowoc
by a buddy's parents' house. We backed the truck
up to the house and knocked.

A heavyset, really cute woman answered.
She had braces but seemed a few years older
than my age of 23. We hit it off right away as I
hauled up items from the basement for her.

Somehow we got on the topic of marijuana; we both wanted to smoke together, so we exchanged numbers.

We finished the hot girl's job with the braces, and I kept getting calls from her. I blew her off a bunch until I was desperate and horny. I was living in West Allis in the trailer and I promised her we would smoke weed at her house 35 miles away in Oconomowoc. I still kept that promise, so I drove back to the jobsite.

She answered the door and smiled. Her braces were gone! The illusion of innocence is gone now! She looked a lot older for some reason; although, I did wait six months to get back to my braces baby.

I felt awkward being there. The businessman in me was telling me this was crossing the line. Not all the other crazy fucking shit I did, but this had me feeling human resources-like.

She was nervous, but in an "I am going to fuck the shit out of you" kinda vibe. I started thinking of her sister and what she would think. "Oh, great my sister fucked the junk guy we hired!" I was getting sweaty and uncomfortable as I packed up a bowl of weed in a really expensive white pipe she possessed. We smoked a while, but I started to feel uncomfortable about fucking a client. The worst part was she was going over her past relationship with a guy with my build and the same age.

It felt like she was preying on me because I was young. I honestly should have fucked her, but at the time it felt really wrong. Something in me made up an excuse and hightailed it out of there.

I remember she was at the door asking, "Are you sure you don't want to stay?" Codeword for "I want to fuck you tonight."

I kindly said "No, thanks" and got back in my Chevy Colorado and left. It still makes me feel good that I pulled out.

Out of Gas

Real Junk Truck review

Name Withheld ★★★★★ 7/3/2012
Wauwatosa, WI

My daughter and son-in-law had just
moved into their first home- had
ripped out carpet, taken down glass
shower doors, and were swamped with
work and not enough hours in a day
to get it all done. I saw and called
this "Big Deal" -- they got back to
me right away and even came sooner
than we'd expected--the next day!
They were great about calling to let
us know they were on the way and
very organized when they arrived.

I was really struggling with my bipolar
disorder. They say that the way you keep your
house is like the inner workings of your mind. My
trailer looked like an episode of hoarders. I would
wake up minutes before my employee for the day
would show up. My phone would be completely
dead from just passing out after getting stoned.
On this day, my employee was Calvin's friend,
Brandon Evans. At the time, Calvin and I were on
bad terms. I had frayed ends of my sanity, and
everyone could tell but me. It is wild that everyone
around you sees you falling apart, but you can't
pick up on it. I went through waves of being aware
of my choices, but also in denial of how much I had
deteriorated mentally.

One problem with working with Brandon was that I had turned into a psychotic maniac. Brandon would pick up on this because he would call me out on my bullshit. I would go into a rage about Calvin, and Brandon would just sit there feeling awkward. I would scream, "I am going to cut off Calvin's head and fuck it." Brandon would be legitimately scared.

The last day Brandon worked for me was the day that we ran out of gas with the Junk Truck on the freeway. It was a very foggy, stormy day. The skies were completely grey like my soul had become. I didn't know it yet, but something very bad was about to take place in my life.

Brandon came to my trailer, and my phone was dead, of course. We left the house in a hurry because I woke up late. We got to the bowling alley where the Junk Truck now was parked because I moved out towards Milwaukee. We fled towards the freeway and drove out of Milwaukee. We made it just out of Milwaukee to Brookfield when I heard, "Sputter! Sputter!" I look at the gas gauge and it's below empty. I feel the truck die and I safely pull over on the freeway. It is pouring out at this point, and I just scream out, "Fuck! Fuck! Fuck!" I am beating my fists against the steering wheel. Brandon looks at me and says, "Dude! You didn't think to check the gas this morning!"

The cab of the truck was always full of random tools and junk, so I grabbed one of the two gas canisters and got out of the truck. Brandon and I jumped this viaduct and walked down the forest area next to the freeway. We were spit out into a neighborhood. We walked to a gas station. The whole time I was screaming violently, "The fucking pigs are gonna get me!"

Brandon just stayed cool while I demeaned law enforcement. I now look back on this and understand that I was in a hypomanic state with my bipolar. We made it back to the freeway once we gassed up. As I went through the forest and back up to jump the viaduct, I was scared for my life because the cars were whizzing by so fast. The worst part was that the gas tank was on the freeway side of the road, so I would have to be in traffic as I knelt down to reach the gas tank.

I was on my knees as cars whizzed past me as I tried to fill the tank. Fuck! The gas can wouldn't fit under the truck! We then had to go back and go to an auto parts store nearby to find a funnel that would fill the truck. When we got back, the police were there to give me assistance. I walked up to an officer and explained my story, and he just looked at me like I was a homeless bum. He scolded me, saying, "Remember to always fill up the night before so this doesn't happen again."

I filled the tank in complete embarrassment. When I got in the truck, the first words out of Brandon's mouth were, "Those cops you just bad-mouthed helped you not get hit by a car."

Honestly, what I remember responding with was, "Fuck the police! I want to shoot a fucking cop!"

Tomb of the Raided

Real Junk Truck review

Name Withheld ★★★★★ 11/11/2018

What a cool service. I was
wondering how I was going to get
some big items out of my basement to
make space for a remodel. They came
on time and got right to work and
worked fast. I was impressed at how
they got the monster tv that lived
in my basement for 20 years out of
the basement. It wowed me. Hard
and smart workers.

It's funny how one moment can change the
course of your entire life. My probation officer,
Vince Totka, always said, "Everyday, you wake up
and walk out the front door. While in public, you
have to make choices; it's up to you to make the
right choices." That is a quote that will always be
burned in my brain.

My life was in shambles. I had moved from
Oconomowoc to a trailer park in West Allis. I was
using more marijuana than ever. My drug use was
making it hard to complete all the daily tasks for
the Junk Truck. My house had clutter everywhere
mixed with unpaid bills that were piling up. The
trailer had a layer of grime that covered every
surface in there.

My daily schedule was to wake up, call to cancel all the jobs, then use marijuana all day just to feel sane. I would usually have my new girlfriend Aspen over to my trailer, so I could go into psychosis and get in an insane screaming match with her. This girl and I had the kind of love that burns maybe too bright for the flame not to die out. I was making the wrong choices and dating the wrong women. My whole family was really worried about me; I was really worried about myself.

My mom saw Mokè in a bar, and he walked up and said, "I miss Travis so much! He got mad at me and stopped talking to me."

My mom stirred her drink and said, "Travis isn't the same person that we once knew." I wasn't acting like myself anymore. My bipolar disorder was taking over my personality. All I could do was feed myself drugs to stay in the mode that I was in.

A few months before this, Calvin had just stopped sleeping at the trailer, so I held his stuff hostage until he paid me his portion of the lot rent. Calvin basically ghosted me after he and his father picked up the rest of his stuff. I remember when they left, I felt comfortable truly losing my mind without a roommate watching.

It was just me and my crazy girlfriend Aspen now. She would be the one to watch The Junk Truck empire crumble. I would smoke a bowl, then I would enter psychosis, and start making crazy demands. One time, I told my girl, "If you don't bring me a honey mustard chicken from Quiznos, you can't come here anymore." The crazy part is that there were no Quiznos left in the area. Knowing this information about the closures made me laugh. There is no way she will show up with a sub from Quiznos. She did! She had a honey mustard chicken sub in her hand when she entered. I thought to myself, "Why am I such an asshole?" I could not stop having psychotic, erratic thoughts. My brain was just spinning out of control.

I was also dealing with my uncle, whose wife left him, and he was spinning out of control, too. All these events were calculated into one big problem. This problem would have to be addressed one way or another. The week before the big event, I sat on my porch, at my trailer, listening to Times of Grace's Hymn of a Broken Man. I sat listening to the album on vinyl and started to break down in tears. I just knew I was in too deep with my mania. There was nothing that could save me from myself. My premonition turned out to be true.

I had gone all week having nervous breakdown after nervous breakdown and I had actually made it alive to Friday. My girl had come over and we had smoked a couple bowls which made both of us tired. Aspen and I wanted to go to Applebee's, but she wanted a quick cat nap. She asked to be woken up when I was dressed to go. Aspen drifted off to sleep. I had been calling my mom and threatening the lives of others. For some reason, I called my mom and told her, "I am going to set my trailer on fire and when the firefighters come, I am going to shoot at them." The funny part of this was that I wasn't a gun owner; no store would ever sell me a gun after the background check came back. My mom got scared and called the West Allis Police. Instead of doing a wellness check, they contacted the West Allis S.W.A.T Team.

I was getting dressed when my Magic Jack phone started to ring. I thought, "That is weird! Nobody has my Magic Jack Number." Magic Jack is a phone that works through the internet, so why would someone be calling me. I never use that software!

The phone started to ring again, so I answered it with curiosity. A man in a serious tone said, "This is so and so from the West Allis Police Department. We need you to step outside and speak with the sergeant."

I explained, "Look I had a bad bipolar day. I am fine really."

The officer said, "It is not an option to not come outside of the trailer. We will be coming to get you otherwise."

I said, "I will come out in a minute."

The second that I opened the door, I saw 10 SWAT officers with shields and machine guns. The officers were in full riot gear. They immediately put a laser sight on my chest. One of the SWAT team officers screamed, "Come off your porch and lay on your stomach." I was basically about to be shot by 10 machine guns, so I stepped off the porch and laid on my stomach. The officers inched little by little to my body. They zip-tied my wrists and loaded me into a squad car.

They immediately asked, "Anyone else in the house?"

I said, "My girlfriend Aspen is sleeping in there; please don't go in there with guns." That statement made one of the pigs go stiff in his cock area; he immediately entered the house to wake Aspen up with a machine in her face.

I started to laugh about how overdramatic my fucking crazy mother is. One of the officers said, "At least you're in good spirits about this raid."

I kept asking, "Do I really need to go somewhere?" They informed me that I needed to go get evaluated by the Milwaukee Mental Health Complex. The crazy part was that the police had no evidence of me making threats, but just because they had heard hearsay, the police were allowed to hold me against my will. Never say this is the land of the free!

The cop took off with me in the back of the squad car and I saw that the police had blocked off every part of the trailer park! There was no fucking escape! The officers would have murdered me if I didn't cooperate. I was about to begin a 10 day journey being locked up inside Wisconsin's most fucked up mental institution.

The Nut House

Real Junk Truck review

Name Withheld ★★★★★ 10/10/2012
Hartland, WI

Hauling away of big item "junk" from
my garage and storage shed.
They hauled away a mattress, an old
grill, and broken furniture. This
was just an easy, great experience.
The guys arrived promptly-even
calling me to let me know EXACTLY
when they would arrive (do you hear
that cable and utility companies??).
It took them less than 30 minutes to
efficiently load all the junk onto
their large truck. These guys are
down-to-earth, nice guys with a
tremendous work ethic. I will
definitely hire them again. I can't
recommend them enough.

The squad car pulled into the intake area
of the Milwaukee Mental Health Complex. My
handcuffs were way too fucking tight, and I kept
complaining about them. The cop said, "We will
take the cuffs off after you are in the intake room."
We waited a half-hour and finally I was brought
into this tiny little intake room.

I had sent someone to the Milwaukee
Mental Health Complex, but I didn't know much
about it. I would learn later that there were some

really shady activities happening at the Complex. They put mentally disabled people with hardened criminals and expected nothing to happen. A young girl with Down syndrome was staying in the same unit as a known serial rapist. Suddenly, the nurses had to give the girl with Down syndrome a pregnancy test. Turns out that the rapist had raped her and got her pregnant! Governor Scott Walker was basically turning a blind eye to the negligence that was taking place at the Mental Health Complex. Sadly, this was going to be my home for the weekend.

Next, they put me in a bullpen with other mentally ill people. I immediately used the phone to call my mom. She answered and I screamed, "I am going to fucking murder you for putting me in here. You know I am going to have to stay the whole weekend now!" My mom basically said she didn't care. I paced around the room in a manic frenzy.

I walked up to this old woman who looked like the world had destroyed her. I took off my shirt and sat next to her. Orderlies ran over to me and told me, "Put your shirt on!"

"Fuck no!" They somehow convinced me to put my garment back on. I waited to speak with a doctor.

I had grown a really big beard by this point and was not showering regularly, so my interview didn't go well because of my aesthetics.

When I was a child, I had a Middle Eastern doctor who turned me into a pill zombie. Ever since then, I am leery of Middle Eastern doctors. When the doctor showed up, you guessed it, he was a Middle Eastern man. I started to have trauma flashbacks to my childhood, but I tried to keep it together. I blurted, "I need a different doctor because of my childhood."

The doctor looked puzzled and asked, "Why?"

I got upset and shouted, "Because I had a bad experience with a Middle Eastern doctor."

Even though I had a childhood traumatic experience, they viewed this as being disorderly. The doctors started to whisper together. I knew I was going to be locked up, so I marched up and said, "I am fine. I just need to go home."

The doctor said, "You don't think you should stay?"

"Fuck no!" I stated my case, "Look I know that I am struggling. I think I might have borderline personality disorder."

He looked at me and said, "Oh, that was the wrong thing to say. Why not get help then?"

They eventually informed me that I was being put on a 72-hour hold. I started to break down in anger. They wanted me to lay down in this room, so I took my shirt off and laid down. The orderly hit the lights and I started ripping the cushion to the point of ruining the couch. I waited in a rage for what seemed like hours until I was let into the unit. I entered the living area which literally looked like a prison. I was shown to my room where this white trash guy that talked all ghetto seemed excited for me to be his roomie. Now, this white trash dude was on so many pills he sorta talked like Sloth from The Goonies, but at this moment I just needed someone to like me in my life.

He left the next night and I got a tall black man as my roommate. He was basketball tall. He had schizophrenia.

The reason this guy was there was that he boarded a bus to Washington, D.C. Once he got there, he went to the white house and walked up to the guards. He informed the secret service that he had a meeting with Barack Obama about business. The secret service realized he obviously was mentally ill and they drove him back to Milwaukee to come to the Complex. He was the best roommate I have ever lived with. I would be reading Garfield comics and he would be talking to invisible people. He would be setting up imaginary business deals with big CEOs of imaginary companies. In a sense, I understood him. I was in so much pain that it felt like I was around my own kind. One night he stood by the window and gazed at the fog that had set in overlooking the courtyard. I could tell that he was deep in thought.

He quietly asked, "Travis, do you smoke weed?"

I didn't know how to respond so I lied and said no.

He shouted, "Good! You will never stop if you do!" Then he went on a rant about the ways he gets women impregnated. He starts going, "I want a direct hit! When I fuck, I go for the direct hit!" I remember laughing my ass off.

My first night there, my cycle of manic episodes had sent me into crash mode. I was asleep right away. Sleeping did me no good because the first thing I did when I got up was go try to find out how I could get out. I walked up to a nurse and said, "I want to see my case manager about how much this stay against my will cost me."

He just shouted, "Go back to your room!" I spit in his face and screamed obscenities at him.

In that moment this old African-American guy walks up and tells me, "Shut the fuck up! I am on the phone."

I screamed, "Shut the fuck up, bitch!" He hit me instantly in the face and the nurses tackled both of us. I screamed at him calling him every name under the sun including vulgar slang. I was carried down the hall by orderlies screaming and kicking back to my room. It was then that something shady happened. They forced me to take pills that knocked me out, but in the meantime, I used the phone to call the police so I could make a statement. I was going to anally fuck this dude by making a statement. The fucking drugs kicked in and I was passed the fuck out. When I awoke in a daze, it was late at night. I immediately went out of my room screaming at the new set of nurses.

I asked, "Where the fuck are the cops? I was beaten up in here today!" They said that this one fat little pig Moesha had sent them away. I was so pissed that again the nurses forced me to take drugs to sleep against my will.

The next morning, I got to eat breakfast in the cafeteria part of the mental prison. I was asked to see the doctor that was handling my case. I looked at this office room that had a group full of people sitting inside. They were psychology students that needed their next subject. I told the nurse, "Look, I am nobody's fucking science project!"

She replied coldly, "You can't get out of here unless the doctor gives the okay."

I ventured inside to find this really attractive twenty-something med student sitting down. I was about to spit right in her face and say,

"Welcome to real life, baby." I decided against it and took my seat. The blonde-haired doctor who looked like his daddy and him used to fuck introduced himself as Dr. Mcvain. He had a scared look in his eyes that told me the whole story. I wasn't getting out! He began to speak, "Travis we are placing you on another 72-hour hold until you can calm down." I got up and shoved the middle finger in his face and left in a rage.

I walked into the lunchroom and just started tossing shit around. The lunchroom had glass windows so the orderlies could see you. Suddenly, a team of security guards came and attacked me. I ended up spitting in one of the nurse's faces. They dragged me into this bare room made up of cinder blocks. In the middle lay a bed with straps. I was shoved on the bed and strapped up by two big nurses. I lay in the bed screaming evil things at the nurses. There was this one nurse that was so evil to me while I was there. She hated me because I was a crazy white guy. That morning, her mother happened to die, so while I was strapped to the bed I said, "I wish I could fuck your mother's corpse!"

She went fucking nuts and said, "You will burn in fucking Hell, cracker."

I giggled and told her, "I am going to break out these straps and murder you!"

She laughed like Cruella DeVille, and said, "No, you won't! You're locked in there, you dumb cracker!" Just as she finished that sentence, I broke out of my first shackle. And started to get up.

She looked like she just saw Chucky with a knife in his hand. She ran off and entered three security guards. One of the guards ran into the room with another shackle in hand. I'm like, "Damn, these guys are prepared." I took more drugs and fell asleep again. It felt like this place was set up to make me crazier.

In the morning, I awoke to this Spanish orderly. I walked up to him and called him a bunch of names and spit on him. This is where something really weird happened. I ran to my room.

He said, "Take Wellbutrin." When I was a kid I had a weird reaction to Wellbutrin, so I informed him of that and his response was, "Take the pill or I am shooting it in your ass." They are never supposed to dispense medication in your room. You take the medication at the front desk while your babysitters watch. I reluctantly swallowed the medication and it knocked me out. I went and took a nap. My girlfriend Aspen once again brought Quiznos that night. My mom stopped by the hospital to visit me again. Some of the people stole my clothes, so I stole someone's black sweater, sat down, and opened my sandwich out of its wrapper.

I started to chat with my mom and Aspen, but I suddenly wasn't feeling right. I don't know what dying feels like, but it was a feeling in my chest that told me the reaper might be nearby. I got up and paced around.

My girl asked, "Are you okay, Travis?"

I took one look at her and bolted out of the lunchroom. I ran into the medical nurses' office. My girl worked at a nursing home and there is a code that comes on over the intercom if someone is about to die. My girl said that code was being shouted over the intercom as one nurse from every department ran to my side. They called an ambulance and I was loaded into it.

The nurses did something that made my heart kind of chill out. As we raced to West Allis Memorial Hospital, the nurse asked me, "What happened?" I told the tale of the nurse drugging me against my will.

He put a stethoscope to my heart and asked, "How do you like taking anti-psychotic medication?"

I said, "I am basically forced against my will or society looks down on me."

He looked at me and said, "Yeah, that medication can be junk in your body." I went to the hospital and immediately got a room because I was basically under arrest. Cops even waited outside my door.

They had sent a nurse to watch over me and make sure I didn't pull an Eric Ross magic stunt. The nurse was very sweet, and she really liked my mom who followed me to the hospital. It was there that I came out of my psychotic break.

She told me, "Travis, you are so funny, but you just need to snap out of this. You could really use your humor for positivity." As I was loaded into the ambulance, I told myself that I was going to get out and take improv comedy classes.

I returned that night a different person than the monster that once lurked within. The next day, a couple of people left and a few newcomers showed up. This one guy came kicking and screaming the night before, and the moment I saw him, I went and called my aunt and said, "Whatever it takes to get me out of here, do it!"

This guy looked like the Slenderman. He had very short dreads on his head. The scary part of him was the way he looked at everyone along with his energy. He looked like he was raping you with eyes every time you made eye contact with him. It was a good thing that I started being on my best behavior before he showed up because he was a person you would never want to be in the real world with. They had put one last 72-hour hold on me, and by this point, I was starting to shape up anyway. I just wanted to go home. I was going to act normal enough for them to let me back into society.

The next morning, I was in the lunchroom for breakfast. The spooky guy was a few tables from me and he was slouched over in his chair looking like a really sleepy gangster. This nurse, named Bear, because he looked like a big teddy, walked up to him and made a motion asking if he was done. The spooky guy asked for milk. Bear replied, "We're not giving out 2 milks for breakfast."

The energy became intense and Bear grabbed him in a bear hug type hold. Mr. Spooky slipped his hands through with a shank in his left hand. Mr. Spooky began stabbing Bear repeatedly in the face with the makeshift shank. Security did break it up but we were told later that Bear was going to need reconstructive surgery on his face. They shoved us all out of the room as Bear laid on his butt covered in blood. I had wished death upon most of the nurses, but Bear was a very good guy who did not deserve what he got.

The next morning, we had art class and I watched Mr. Spooky color in a picture of a bunny with colored markers. It was quite the contrast from the bloodbath the day before. We were all asked what our goal was. My goal was to get healthy enough to get out of this place. Mr. Spooky had a really crazy response to his goal. Mr. Spooky said, "I want to go to prison. That is where you are truly free!"

165

I remember thinking that was so bizarre, so I asked him, "Why would you want that?"

He replied, "Once you are locked up, you are truly free because they can't do anything else to you!" At the time I thought that statement was crazy talk, but after years of being beaten down by life, I think I truly get what Mr. Spooky meant. In some way, what Mr. Spooky said is quite poetic. Life can beat you down and sometimes people just don't get up anymore.

After the last 72-hour hold was done, Dr. Mcvain reluctantly let me go back home. I had missed tons of potential jobs and the 10 day stay had cost me roughly 20,000 dollars. It's funny to me they can force you against your will to stay somewhere; meanwhile, they charge you thousands of dollars to be a prisoner.

I immediately got home and pulled an ounce of marijuana out of the freezer. I started smoking some really strong imported weed. I was looking for something in the drawer when I found a needle in my drawer. My girlfriend Aspen was a recovering heroin addict, and she had been having people over and doing heroin with them in my trailer. It really broke my fucking heart. I hate to see people go down that path. I also had a feeling like my car had just been broken into, hypothetically. By her using heroin and having men over to my house, it left me feeling very violated. She immediately told me that she was leaving and rushed out. I promised not to tell her parents that she relapsed. I just told her that she needed to get help and she blamed her relapse on my nervous breakdown.

We broke up soon afterwards because we just couldn't stop fighting. It took me almost a decade to recover from the house being raided. Everything from my finances to my housing, I had to rebuild my entire life.

The World's Greatest Junk Parade

Going to the Milwaukee Mental Health Complex will always be one of my saddest memories. I feel that I need a breather from the wreckage of my past, so I am going to discuss one of my favorite aspects of the business right now. One of the happiest memories from my junk removal career was the Junk Parade that passed through the Sullivan and Rome townships of Jefferson County. The parade is what you think it is; it's a push, pull, and drag of junk vehicles and floats made of rubbish. People from all over come and sit on the county road to watch the junk roll down the street.

The first year I did the parade was kind of on a whim. It was 2011, My mother had told me about the parade, and I had an old trailer in my parents' yard to decorate with junk. We saved junk from a few jobs and stored them in my parents' garage.

That weekend, I strung junk all over my truck and trailer. I ended up putting an exercise bike on the hood of the Junk Truck. I strung Christmas stuff on the truck for the labor day junk fiasco. My mom was going to drive the truck in the parade with her friend Joan in the passenger seat. I invited Nate Schwantz, Mark Drawn, and Calvin White to the parade with me.

We took off that day with no one in the exercise bike on the hood of the Junk Truck. It was exhilarating to be cruising in our Junk Truck full of rubbish. At one point, one junk float caught fire and the parade had to be stopped so the fire department could put out the flames. My mom called out for Nate to jump on the hood and juggle some balls. Nate, in a sombrero, hopped on the bike to juggle his heart out.

That first year, we didn't know the parade had judges that gave out awards, so that first year was just about fun.

The second year, I was in it to win it, so I called in a few favors from friends. I was going to have my friend Mark Ant play the sax to the tune of the Sanford and Son theme; meanwhile, Nate was going to juggle fire this time on the exercise bike on top of the hood. My friend Mark Drawn would be there again. That week in junk removal, we got boxes of cheesy, grocery store romance novels. My plan was to pass out the romance novels to the adoring crowd.

The day of, we pulled into the park to stage our junk floats with the other piles of shit. Mark Ant, of course, showed up late and didn't know the song to Sanford and Son. It was the early days of smartphones, but I pulled out my brick and looked up the song on YouTube and played the song for him to memorize. My mom and Joan were in their Junk Truck shirts ready to roll with the junk float.

The local news TMJ4 was there to cover the Junk Parade, so I made myself available to shamelessly promote The Junk Truck. I was really nervous, but I pulled off the on-camera interview. In the background, Nate was juggling fire on the exercise back attached to the hood. Later that night, we saw that they used Mark's saxophone playing as the backtrack to the news piece.

We pulled out and started the parade route. I was running on the side of the truck trying to pass out all the romance novels. We had saved the steamy supermarket novels just so we could be quirky at the junk parade. Nate was Juggling fire on the hood. My girlfriend Nora was throwing out candy with Calvin White and Mark Drawn.

I tried to pass out the romance novels to old women, and the trick worked. The old ladies loved the gag gift! At one point, the parade stopped, and Nate dropped the flame stick under my Junk Truck. The problem was that the Junk Truck had a bad exhaust leak. Nate screamed when it rolled under because he knew that the truck could blow up. I quickly rolled under the truck and got the flame stick. It was a relief to not have the fire department have to put out my blazing truck.

As we got to the judges, I jumped up on their podium and handed each judge a romance novel. At the after-party, we found out we won third place. Nate, Mark, Calvin, and I all smoked pot in the back of the Junk Truck to celebrate mediocrity. Smoke was pouring out the wooden sides of the stake bed truck, as my mom was freaking out that we were getting high. My new girlfriend Nora's mom was against the inhalation of Mary Jane, so I was taking a big risk in our relationship by smoking. I didn't give a fuck! We spent our high throwing toilets from great distances in the back of the Junk Truck. Mark Ant ended up missing the bed of the truck with the toilet. The shitter shattered and it cut my girlfriend Nora on her hand badly. I quickly grabbed a first aid kit and had a beautiful moment taking care of my girl. At the end of the day, Mark Drawn looked at me and said, "next year we are going to win this thing."

The third parade we took so fucking seriously. We wanted to be Junk Kings and sit on the throne of Junk Parade Mountain. I have to give the entire credit of the float idea to Mark Drawn. His idea was to make the whole float an instrument almost like a Stomp-type performance. Mark enlisted the help of his drummer friends and we went to town wiring pots, pans, and other hittable junk on the trailer. Mark Drawn and I spent an entire Saturday planning and building our life-size junk drum set. Calvin and Nate were both out of commission for this year's float, so it ended up being a cast of Mark Drawn's friends.

The day came, and I was nervous that the drummers might not show up to play on the trailer's junk drums. Some great Wisconsin musicians named Steve Zoona and Fernando showed up with Mark Drawn.

171

This was going to be great! Again, my mom and Joan would drive the rig; meanwhile, The Junk Truck Players would bless the crowd with rhythm. People also went nuts for our can koozies.

Again, we took off in the rubbish float, but this time it felt different. Fernando, Steve, and Mark had some really funky beats going that were making the crowd move and groove. It felt like we might actually win the World's Greatest Junk Parade. I walked on the side of the truck to give the kids candy. As the truck drove down the parade route, the guys would change up the beats every so often to not seem mundane. It was cool to hear all of the sounds that the pots, pans, and various junk made. We approached the judge's podium and I witnessed all the judges' bodies feeling the music. They were moving and grooving!

We pulled into the after-staging area and I was excited to see what the results would be. The results were announced with the three winners. First, was the best Company float, next was the best float. Both announcements didn't read, "The Junk Truck". My heart was pounding because we hadn't won a trophy.

The judge said, "The next trophy is for judges' choice and we wanted to award it to someone that has been here every year. This individual really worked hard every year to improve their float. The judges' choice is The Junk Truck". I was stunned! I ran right up to the podium, grabbed my award, and started speaking into the microphone. I was shaking in my voice as I explained what The Junk Truck offered in its junk removal service. I held my trophy high as I watched all my friends and family cheer me on. As stupid as this sounds, it was one of the most beautiful moments of my life. I got off stage and Mark Drawn said he was proud of me for saying where they could find The Junk Truck. Winning the World's Greatest Junk Parade was a crowning achievement in my throwaway life.

The Jerk Off

I had hired this skeevy guy that I went to high school with. We will call him Yellow Teeth because he is a huge piece of shit (oh, and he has yellow teeth). All the time I've known him, if I dated a hot girl for a while, I don't know what it is, but Yellow Teeth would go behind my back and fuck her. Yellow Teeth must love being where my penis has been!

In high school, Yellow Teeth would glue his hair to be punk and wear clothes that were too tight for his chubby, slob body. In his thirties, he played in this Milwaukee band where they played children's toys in the band. Literally nobody liked his band. It was music that 4 or 5 people in the entire world might like. He also got engaged to literally any girl that he dated because he was so ugly and desperate. Later on in The Junk Truck, I hired him because I thought he might not be a dick, but the second that I lost the company, he treated me like I was a murderer. He really loved to kick me when I was down. After The Junk Truck closed, I asked him for a job at the head shop he worked at. Yellow Teeth rolled his eyes and said, "We need someone with experience."

I gave the fucker an opportunity when he needed it and he shamed me at the lowest point in my life by not getting me a job when a position opened up. Against my will, my mom put the title of his car in her name because he had such outstanding debts that he couldn't afford his own insurance. It always really bothered me that he was on my mom's insurance, but my drunk mother for some reason would let it go on. My mom would say, "But Yellow Teeth pays on time!" It was just another way after The Junk Truck ended that Yellow Teeth could stomp me while I was down!

Later on, after I left a horrible relationship, I confided in Yellow Teeth what had happened. He turned around and started fucking my crazy ex, Ava! He is obviously happy being able to rape me at every turn. My ex that now fucks him used to call him Yellow Teeth behind his back, so we will call him that going forward.

Mistaken Identity

Real Junk Truck Review

Name Withheld ★★★★★ 7/30/2012
Milwaukee, WI

We had an Angie's List coupon.
Travis and his partner Matt hauled
some very heavy, bulky furniture out
to the truck. Travis and Matt were
very efficient. They were careful
not to scratch the walls or the
doors as they were hauling this
furniture out of the house. They
were professional and personable.
They wanted to know if there was
anything else they could do for us.
My wife and I were very impressed.
We will use them again in the
future.

My panic attacks and manic rages were on
point during the end of me owning the company. I
felt like I was sweating my bed in a constant
nightmare owning and operating a junk removal
business. My mom had taken over the phone
duties because I was having panic attacks, blind
rages, and psychosis. On this day, all I had was
an estimate to do in Pewaukee. The Lake Country
area has weird addresses starting in W-
something and N-something etc., so I was having
a hard time finding the address. I have to be
honest and admit that I was calling my mom

exploding in a fucking downward spiral. I kept telling my mom, "I am just fucking going fucking home! FUCK THIS!"

I was bashing my fists against the steering wheel and screaming bloody murder. I kept driving back and forth down the same fucking street. At one point, a car with an older couple drove by. They gave me a look, so I flipped them off waving my middle finger around like it's a wand.

I called my mom screaming that I am fucking leaving, and she said that the customers called and were waiting. I don't remember how I found the house, but I was pleasantly surprised to find that the couple that I flipped off on the way were the customers who were looking for an estimate!

I was like, "Fuck!" I turned in the driveway to face the music. I was shaking as I stepped out of the car; The couple had smiles on their faces; They greeted me with cheer! They turned out to be a very nice couple with a big old house to clean out. As I walked with them, I kept choking on my words because of how embarrassed I was. I was acting like a thief who just robbed an old lady, but was now helping walk her across the street. I gave them my quote and they seemed excited to work with me, but I ended up never sending in my estimate because I was too busy getting high and being a lazy ass. Oh, what could have been...

NO, DAD!

Real Junk Truck Review

Name Withheld ★★★★★ 10/22/2012
La Crosse, WI

Hauled away large cardboard, a pallet, and carpet. Swept the garage where the materials had been stored, too.

Excellent experience! Professional, prompt, and personable. The price was very fair. The owner asked if we were satisfied with their work before submitting the bill. Will undoubtedly use in the future! One of the best service providers I've used from Angie's List.
Thank you so much!!!!!

By this time, I was being consumed by junk removal. I was beyond burned out and hated my customers. I started to get an attitude about going to jobs and started to have panic attacks about driving the truck. I would lay in my bed under the covers just hoping time would stand still. I prayed that I wouldn't have to drive the truck. The problem was that I had to keep going. My mom set me up with a customer out near Waterford that could only do a job on a Saturday. Waterford is a town way out of our service range; it would be hard to service his needs because of the distance between Waterford and the dump.

The guy had a humongous storage unit that needed to be cleaned out. The annoying part was that I only had one truck to fill with junk and the dump closed at noon. The guy insisted on 10 AM for the start of the job, so the guy somehow thought I might be the second coming of Christ, and expected me to snap my fingers and the junk would disappear. This customer expected me to be able to clean out the whole unit in two hours! I was already in a bad fucking mood driving out to this unit because I couldn't stand how customers think we are miracle workers.

Yellow Teeth and I showed up to a ghetto, rundown storage unit surrounded by gravel. I pulled up and the first words out of the customer's mouth were, "That's an awfully small truck for this job!"

I fucking clenched my fists in a complete rage because of how fucking sick I was of hearing that exact phrase. Do people expect us to drive up in a semi-trailer? I basically just told him off by saying that my mom explained that we told him ahead of time about the dumping situation. The guy wanted us to load as much junk as possible. The man was all about trying to rid himself of everything in the unit, but he had brought his pony-tailed, loser son with him to help out. The customer's son was a little bitch from the get-go. His son looked like he lived with daddy, worked at daddies business, and still sucked on his mommy for milk. The whole unit was filled with just complete rubbish. Everything from a gross old cooler to old plumbing supplies that were in one giant heap of pure bullshit.

Every piece of crap we pulled out to throw in the truck, Ponytail would literally shout, "Dad, no!" Then, he would give an explanation on why they needed that certain item of garbage. Honestly, it got so ridiculous that if we would have pulled out his mother's bloody tampons, he would have had a reason like, "Dad, no! That tampon holds blood from my mother's cunt and that is where I came out of!"

Every turd possession that we threw in the truck, the bitch son screamed, "No, dad!" The father kept yelling at the loser that everything was garbage. Yellow Teeth and I thought it was funny to agitate the son, so we started heaving everything into the truck faster. The son had to walk away in a pouty temper tantrum over this rubble of undesirables. I hated my job so much, but it was so satisfying to see this middle-aged, basement-dwelling dweeb lose his shit like a child. I am a man of my word, so I loaded up a full load in the Junk Truck, I shook hands with Dad, and we took off back to Milwaukee. On the way home, we kept mocking the son by screaming, "No, Dad!" Just know that all junk men mock their customers when they throw tantrums over crap.

So Long, Old Friend

I was saving up to buy a house, living back at the lakehouse on Lower Nehbabin. My stepdad was turning against me and my then-girlfriend Ava. He wanted us out because I had spent all summer smoking weed by my super hot pepper garden. My stepdad was also actively trying to cheat on my mom. He would buy Fleshlights and look at Adult Friend Finders. We caught him looking at demented porn and having cock rings sent to the house. When my stepdad would cheat on my mom, he would use an online alias of the name Dylan.

I really wanted to clean up the yard because I had bought a house and was waiting to close. First, I took all the rubbish that was always too hard to get rid of. Now that the yard was clean, I put my trailer for sale that I never used. Lastly, sadly, I put my mean green machine for sale. I ended up selling it to a tow truck because it was a 1986 and so much time had passed since starting the company that no one had a need for an old truck like that.

I was heavily involved in improv comedy at the time. I had an improv practice in Milwaukee that I didn't want to miss, which was good because I couldn't bear to see my old friend take off on me. My mom showed me pictures of it driving away with a beautiful red, pink, and purple sunset in the background. I still think of that truck to this day; it

181

makes me sick that I don't have it anymore. Until
we meet again big green...

Accidents and Phone Books

Real Junk Truck review

Name Withheld ★★★★★ 8/30/2012
Shorewood, WI

I purchased the $79 special. I
called the Junk Truck on a Saturday.
Travis returned my call the same
day, and we arranged for him to haul
away a number of boxes of old files,
financial records, etc. from the
attic. He was available on the date
and time I requested even though it
was fairly short notice. He gave me
a one-hour window for his arrival,
and he arrived within that time
frame, which I greatly appreciated.
He and an employee made quick work
of removing the boxes even though by
midafternoon that day the temp had
risen to 90 degrees making the attic
very hot. The service was prompt,
professional, and courteous.

See above. I was very pleased with
their service. I would definitely
use their service again, and I plan
to recommend their service to
others.

Around the time that Yellow Teeth started working for me, two really weird incidents happened, the first being Yellow Teeth's birthday.

Yellow Teeth and I were pulling into this neighborhood on his birthday. The neighborhood was all well-kept upper-middle-class homes. We were in the truck admiring the houses. You can always tell a customer's house by usually guessing that the most ratchet house will be your destination. This was no different, the rows of nice houses had one at the end that looked like a storm cloud hovered above the house permanently. The house looked like something out of a horror movie where the house is possessed. Weeds had overtaken the entire property in the midst of upper-class suburbia.

I was afraid to go up to the door in fear that the vines in the yard would come to life and grab me. I looked at Yellow Teeth and we both had concerned looks on our faces. This short little Asian woman answers the door with a very thick accent. It was hard to understand what she wanted as I listened very intently. She showed Yellow Teeth and me around. What we saw was horrifying. She brought us into this room that had old green and white tiles. Some were broken. The room had big clunky metal desks standing up. The chilling part was that she had wet phone books that were growing into the floor. The phone books had a green slime membrane casing around the books. It was like there was some evil monster that birthed a phone book and it was the wretched spawn of Lucifer.

She showed us a living room that was filled with boxes and a really old black and white television. The house had yellow curtains that were thought to be once stunning white. She had the curtains hanging off, so half the room had orange sun bursting through. The lady moved fast through the house just rambling about nothing.

This lady was obviously mentally ill because she just acted so strange. She kept babbling on and on. The lady would go to one part of the house and show me one item in a room filled to the brim with junk. Then, she would show us one item on the opposite side of the house. This made me feel for her in a deep way. I am mentally ill myself, and I would never take money from a mentally ill person that isn't present or in reality. I am not shady like that. Sadly, the old lady was very mentally ill and I needed her son to be there to assure me that I wasn't taking advantage of her. The house itself was a hoarding apocalypse which means it might have cost over $10,000 to clean up. I informed the lady that I would come back when her son was there since he set up the appointment. She just wasn't in reality, and it didn't feel right unless I had validation she wanted the cleanout. It was really scatterbrained, so Yellow Teeth and I got out of there.

When we got back in the truck, I told Yellow Teeth, "I would never make you do a cleanout like that on your birthday!"

With excitement and relief, Yellow Teeth said, "Thank you!"

A few weeks later, Yellow Teeth and I were pulling the Junk Truck into an apartment complex in Kenosha. The city is very pretty, but it is very blue-collar; the town is filled with a lot of taverns and liquor stores. As I turned, this woman tried to get around me on the right side and T-boned us. It was hysteria when we got out of the truck. The worst part was that the customer was watching from her porch! This old, plump woman called out, "Are you boys alright?"

A young woman and young man got out of the red SUV and looked upset. I started to scream at Yellow Teeth, "They fucking hit me! I am going to sue them!" My hope was that would scare them off from reporting the accident. The Junk Truck was fine, so I needed them to just go.

The guy looked at his girl and said to me, "Hey man, we don't want any trouble, so we are just going to go." I was very angry but nodded my head yes. They took off in the now smashed-up red SUV. We then turned the attention to our customer.

We took down a sleeper couch for the lady and she ranted and raved about how good our service was! I thought to myself, "Maybe we should get in an accident every day..." The plump, old lady told us that she had a big cleanout for us because her husband was transitioning to be disabled.

When the job took place, it was winter and there was light dusting of snow on the ground. I had lined up my uncle Jared to do the cleanout with me. My uncle Jared is one of the laziest people I know. He had a "motorcycle shop" in his garage which was code word for smoking weed all day and taking a few months to finish a person's bike. By the time the customer got their bike back, the summer for riding was over. My uncle would find any excuse to get out of helping me with junk removal, but his wife demanded that they needed the extra cash. This time was no different. I got a call from Jared that went like this.

"Hello?"

"Hey Travis, it's Jared, look I won't be able to get to the job because of the snow. I have to shovel my driveway."

"Jared! It snowed a light dusting! Just get here now!" Jared refused to show up, so I lost the plump woman who saw me get hit as a customer. All because Jared couldn't shovel the centimeter of snow that covered his driveway. What a fucking dickhead!

Pizza Guy

Real Junk Truck review

Name Withheld ★★★★★ 9/7/2012
Milwaukee, WI

I hired the company to remove two
sofas: one a hide-a-bed and one a
love seat. The hide-a-bed was a
full-size sofa which had been a
challenge to deliver. Also, my
apartment is small so access to the
doors was very tight. Both sofas
were dusty and covered with pet
hair. They also removed a large old
portable dishwasher. I have some
additional items in my basement. I
will be calling The Junk Truck to
remove them in the near future

The Junk Truck company advertised an
"Angie's List Big Deal". After I
read the reviews, their reviews and
looked up several other hauling
companies I selected The Junk Truck.
A big part of my decision was based
on their good recycle/reuse program.
The truck with two workers arrived
on time (actually a few minutes
early). They looked over the items
and then promptly began to remove
them. They were very careful to move
other furniture around my items
without damaging anything including

the outer doors which are narrow and
could have presented a problem.

Towards the end of me owning the Junk
Truck, I was doing jobs periodically for a hoarder.
He resembled Will Ferrell doing an impression of
Harry Carey; he even talked like it, too. For some
reason, he would only want to do jobs when his
wife was away at work. His wife was a mysterious
character that worked long shifts at a rat poison
factory.

The house was like an episode of Hoarders
with little tunnels of junk that lead from room to
room. They had 2 big German Shepherds that
were always caged up because they would bark
viciously at me, wanting my blood. While we
cleared out piles of junk, the guy would ask us in a
Harry Caray-type voice, "What kind of pizza do
you like?" We had several visits with this guy, and
he always needed to know what our favorite pizza
joints were every time! I never got an answer on
why he asked every time. The gentleman was just
a fan of marinara.

His house would get cleared out with every
visit, but as soon as it started getting around 2:30,
he would get anxious about his wife coming home
to us. Junk removal teams are the Devil's work
through a hoarder's eyes.

Now about the junk, he had items that his
wife hoarded from Target, mixed with clothes,
mixed with pellets of rat poison.

It was extremely sad to know that animals were living around rat poison pellets. You could tell that the guy loved the two German Shepherds, and his heart was in the right place, but the environment was no place for animals.

The dogs would just sit in the cages and bark viciously at me as I walked past with some junk. One of the latches on the cage was broken, so I would always be scared they would get out. The dogs didn't seem friendly to strangers.

Another weird hoarding aspect to them was that they hoarded jars of change. They had closets full of jars of change; there must have been thousands in coin form. They had change and money just laying around. I would hand the man a 20 dollar bill and say, "Don't let this go in the truck!"

He would laugh and continue talking about pizza or he would talk about pro wrestling. I would be talking wrestling storylines with him as I would watch the 20 I just gave him fall back onto the floor with the rest of the rubbish. All in all, the pizza guy was one of my most cherished clients that I ever had with The Junk Truck. He was a soft, gentle guy that was basically an encyclopedia of professional wrestling. It was fascinating to watch him talk about wrestling and pizza. It was a pure joy to help Pizza Guy rid himself of his hoarding habits.

Something About Hot Tubs

Real Junk Truck review

Name Withheld ★★★★★ 9/26/2012
Bayside, WI

I used them to haul away a hot tub
that was broken. They came on time,
quickly cut it up, and loaded it.
They also took some extra wood that
needed to go without any additional
cost. I have used them in the past
and like their work ethic.

I hated the Junk Truck by this point. I was
just going through the motions to get home so I
could smoke weed, relax, and not have panic
attacks. My anxiety was through the roof. I wasn't
even living in the moment anymore; I was living a
day ahead because after all, I would have to get
up and drive the death machine down the road,
just hoping that the truck wouldn't malfunction.
The new truck was having mechanical issues and
it was starting to be a liability to drive that blue
truck around. I bought the blue truck after I had to
retire the original green truck I used. The problem
now was that the blue truck was becoming out of
service. It was not road safe, but I drove it. I would
just jam the stick into the gears to get from point A
to point B just to get the day over with.

191

With this death machine, I took off with Yellow Teeth to do a job out in Sussex, Wisconsin. We got to a decently sized house in a subdivision. This younger, blonde in her 20's showed us where the hot tub was.

The hot tub was on the ground with a deck built around it. There was no place to make cuts to get rid of the hot tub. I gathered in a corner and asked Yellow Teeth, "Do you think that we can do this?"

"I don't know, man! The deck is basically covering the hot tub."

At this point, I was thinking The Junk Truck has seen it all, so we will figure out a way to cut this hot tub up. We turned to the girl and told her we would start work. We busted out our Milwaukee Sawzall and started to make cuts without much progress. They didn't want the deck cut into which was making this basically impossible. Fiberglass foam was now blowing around in their suburban setting.

At one point, we tried to get under the deck but it had lattices that prevented us from accessing the tub. We kept making cuts while making a huge mess. I have to be honest with myself. I gave up. I just wanted to go home and smoke weed. I ended up just knocking on the door and informing the girl that the tub wouldn't be able to come out unless they cut part of the deck (which was true).

The girl was confused and angry. She asked, "Did you guys not bring the right equipment?"

We left in a hurry to escape the awkward moment of, "I just fucked your house up, homeowner bitch."

A few days later my mom called me and said, "Please, don't get mad but that hot tub lady complained to the Better Business Bureau." We read the complaint and the husband of the girl said that they had 3 or 4 different companies come to look at the hot tub and none of them would touch it because of the way it had a deck built around it. These fucking people called enough companies until one was stupid to attempt it (me). I was fucking furious and they were demanding that I show back up to finish the hot tub.

Now, I was ashamed, but sometimes in business you can't just smoke, you actually have to suit up and show up. The husband took off a few boards so we could saw the tub. We came back and the girl was waiting for me, we sawed up the tub, and went on our merry way. Looking back, my head wasn't in the game anymore and that is when mistakes happen.

Barky's Lakeside

In any business, you seem to always be chasing your customers to get paid for past jobs. Usually, when someone would skip town and not pay, I would file to put a lien on their house. Once the paperwork would get sent to the homeowner, they would always come calling to pay me my money. That routine usually would work with anyone. Except for this one time, it took years to see my money.

We did an estimate for a pub that was on Okauchee Lake. I just bought my Chevy Colorado because the owners said it was just fridges. I backed my truck up to the bar and was greeted by some shady barkeep. He was short, stocky, wearing a black polo. He looked like a Vegas bouncer. He brought us down to the basement and showed us one residential deep freezer and one giant commercial freezer. I didn't feel comfortable moving the commercial freezer with just me and Yellow Teeth. He felt the same, so I informed the barkeep. I told him we would just move the smaller one because I only had one guy with me. The barkeep seemed pissed but agreed.

The deep freezer glided up the giant wood-stained steps. Next, I went in for payment, but the barkeep said the owner would cut the check at a later date. I told him we needed payment on the spot, but he said his hands were tied.

We sent an invoice… and sent an invoice… then another invoice….. My mom just kept sending out invoices like clockwork. We ended up sending invoices for the next two years. In those years, a lot changed with our company. I could have desperately used that money.

It seemed like we would never recoup that measly $115. Word started to get around that Barky's Lakeside wasn't paying their employees, vendors, or paying their taxes. Disgruntled employees started to create hoopla on Facebook. They were demonizing the owner who we will call Rick. It felt like this would be the only opportunity to get my money back. The word all over town was that the government was going to shut the restaurant down because of their financial delinquency. The feds were looking into the day-to-day of the business because of not paying employees, gypping vendors, and avoiding taxes.

My mom just kept saying she was going to get me my money in Hell or high water. My mom is a really tough cookie that has made people pick up and move after they have pissed her off. One time, my aunt by marriage cheated on my uncle. She just so happened to be an NBA dancer for the Milwaukee Bucks. My mom made such a stink that the Milwaukee Bucks feared my mom's wrath, so I didn't doubt that my money would eventually show with my stone-cold mom on my side.

My mom wanted to confront the owner sooner than later because he could just claim bankruptcy leaving us with zero. My mom's boyfriend Roller wanted to accompany her to the bar. My mom went to the bar to find that the owner wasn't there, but his girlfriend was tending the bar. My mom walked up to her and said, "Have your boyfriend call me so we can get this 2-year-old bill paid!"

She called him and he must have asked if she was really standing in front of her because she whispered on the phone, "They are standing right in front of me." The girlfriend got off the phone with him and said that the owner didn't know anything about a bill from The Junk Truck.

My mom put her foot down and said, "I am not leaving this bar without my son's money!" My mom then started going around to different tables full of customers telling them about their shady business practices. My mom then circled back to the bar and said, "I can stay here all night and tell every customer why I am here." My mom's boyfriend started to feel embarrassed about my mom's actions, but my mom didn't give a fuck. My mom then spat out, "It's only $115."

The bartender didn't want a big scene, so she asked for my mom's number so that the owner could personally call her. My mom said, "Fine, but if he doesn't call me, I'll be back." My mom retreated to her truck. Sure enough, a call came through my mom's phone. An apple must have fallen on the owner's noggin because he suddenly remembered the job that The Junk Truck did!

He told my mom "I don't believe that I should have to pay because you only took one fridge!" It's funny how he remembered us now. My mom informed him that he would still have to pay for the removal of the one fridge. He told my mom, "Walk back in the bar and my girlfriend will pay $115 out of the register." Two weeks later, the feds shut down Barky's and they were sued by their employees and vendors.

Good Luck Chuck

Real Junk Truck review

Name Withheld ★★★★★ 6/19/2012

The Junk Truck did a great job
cleaning out the years of junk I had
accumulated through the years. They
were efficient and friendly. I
would use them again.

I had this fill-in employee, he was Yellow Teeth's roommate. This guy looked like if Charlie Brown grew up and smoked and drank every day for all of his Peanuts youth. He worked at a head shop on the East Side of Milwaukee. This guy sold weed on and off and was obsessed with computer games. Everyone called him Brownie because of his resemblance to the comic book character. Brownie just needed a couple of hours a week for extra cash. He was finishing up a business degree at UWM, so he liked to hop in the truck and give me business advice that I didn't fucking want. I was just going through the motions at this time in my life. I was beaten down by life. I was trying to buy my first house, so I could have a place to lay my head as I went through my bipolar problems. The plan was to secure my house so I could take a breather in life.

I was being forced to take these first-time homeownership classes the weekend that Brownie and I had some jobs. A customer called and said, "I only have one truckload of stuff." I was relieved but concerned that the customer was lying. Customers almost love to lie to themself about how much junk they actually have to get rid of. The customer was flying in from New York to clean out her old house.

We got to the customer's house and met with a lady who was short and plump with brunette hair. She took us inside, and said, "This is it! Take everything in the house!" *Ugh...* the house looked like it had been stuffed with junk for the last 30-40 years.

I giggled inside and said, "We were scheduled to load up one truck. It is Saturday and the dumps close at noon." She looked horrified as I told her, "I won't be able to do any work here because I have already committed to First Time Home Buyers classes this Sunday. We also would have nowhere to dump any of this junk!" The lady looked like I just told her that she had stage 4 cancer.

The woman angrily said, "What am I supposed to do?"

The answer in my head was, "I don't give a fuck what you do. You fucking told me you had one fucking truckload of stuff, but instead, you have 16 loads to take out! I don't give a fuck what you do!" My real answer was, "I don't know. You only told me you had one truckload. Sorry, I don't have the manpower to even get this house cleaned out."

It was super awkward as Brownie and I packed up. I wished the lady good luck as her head was spinning with fear. She had to be out of there, but I just didn't give a fuck anymore. Sometimes I think of that client. She probably still thinks of me as she thinks of a horrible contractor experience, but I still don't give a fuck...

College Skunks

Real Junk Truck review

Name Withheld ★★★★★ 1/26/2012
Fox Point, WI

Needed to have old paneling,
drywall, screens, and shutters
hauled away. They did a great job.
They showed up on time, gave me an
estimate, and started to work
immediately. Most of the material
was outside, but they also needed to
go up to the garage rafters for the
screens and shutters. Did all of it
in under an hour and when there was
less material than the original
estimate, they reduced the price.
They are professional and courteous
and the pricing is reasonable,
especially compared to the franchise
companies. Great job and I would
recommend.

I didn't give a fuck about the Junk Truck at
this point, but jobs kept rolling in. It was starting to
feel like I was playing chicken with a train. I felt like
I would derail mentally again to the point of
committing myself. When I first saw that homeless
junk guy in cut-off jeans at the Catholic thrift
store, I wanted to be him because he was a bum.
After I started the business, I wanted to
professionalize junk removal in Wisconsin. Sadly, I
had turned into that homeless guy that was

glistening in the sun long ago. The role was reversed now, I had turned into a drug zombie who hauled boards up from basements. I wasn't an owner; I was just another junk slave. At this point I wasn't smoking weed anymore; weed was smoking me. Mistakes were being made more and more to the point that I was beginning to mess up on jobs. I wasn't damaging walls; I was damaging my reputation. One occasion in particular was pretty damaging.

Yellow Teeth sold weed, so on the way to the job we stopped at his house, and I bought an 8th. We hopped in my Chevy Colorado to just pick up one washer. I had forgotten to take the weed out. The weed was extremely stinky as it sat in my jacket pocket.

We got to Shorewood and backed the truck up into the driveway, knocked on the door, and an older gentleman with Ben Stein glasses answered the door. We stepped inside and as the door closed it smelled like a skunk. It was early spring, so it was still cold in Wisconsin. The gentlemen had his furnace blasting and once he closed the door, the perfume of Marijuana lingered in the foyer.

I knew right away that it was the herb Yellow Teeth that sold me. The tension was building in this awkward situation. You could just feel the customer's dismay in the air; it's almost what he didn't say to us that made things worse. Reluctantly, he led us down to the basement, we picked up the washer and hauled it up the stairs.

One positive aspect of junk jobs these days was that I wasn't having appliances tumble down the stairs on someone. I had reached journeyman status since the days of Mr. Good Guy. It was loaded into my truck in ten minutes, and the payment on his card went through. He awkwardly said goodbye to us. Yellow Teeth said, "You really screwed up back there, man!" I absolutely screwed up every aspect of my life; part of me was comfortable living in chaos and shambles.

Dirty Dousman

A really tragic part of junk removal is cleaning out hoarding houses of alcoholics and dealing with the families who love them. You really see how tragic addiction is to families all over. One case of hoarding that I dealt with was in a town right outside of Oconomowoc called Dousman. The town mascot is a frog because of the wildlife that lives around there. The town also has a really bad mosquito problem.

We were called out through the years to this dilapidated old house with a long, gravel driveway. The driveway was so overgrown with vegetation that the Junk Truck would be rifled with branches against the side of the truck. A very nice woman met us and took us inside a very sad situation. The very nice woman was the sister of the guy who lived there. He was always in the hospital when we would try to clear out a few rooms over a weekend. The house was unlivable. The mattress that this guy would sleep on had black grime that made an imprint of the shape of a body. The house had passages to get from room to room. Each room had huge junk piles in it, but all the piles were covered in a layer of dust that I couldn't believe was real. Orange cat hair covered every inch of the house like Garfield had been his drinking buddy.

The first room we cleaned out was the living room area. The living room had bookshelves that were wall-to-wall encyclopedias and National

Geographic magazines. The whole truck ended up being full of books, magazines, and Brain Quest.

Next, we went to the alcoholic's room. There was a cigarette butt shrine in a corner of the room. The grime on all his stuff was uncanny. You have to hold your breath even with the mask on. His blankets were crusty with cum. We filled that second load that day hoping we had made a difference, but the next time we came back, the rooms were full again.

We learned that the sister lived in New York and would come up to try to clean the house out, so the house could be put up for sale. The brother would have other addicts live with him and they would use together and live in shambles. Hearing this really woke me up to my own mental illness. The family's story also reminded me how fragile life is. Substances can change your brain chemistry and emotions, turning you into an addict. Taking decades off of your life; wasting of your life.

Over the years, we helped the family clean out the home until finally, the woman felt she could not enable her brother any longer. She kicked him out of the house she let him stay in. I had sold The Junk Truck to my mom by now and was bitter and angry about my life situation. We had to do one last cleanout at the Dousman Booze House. My mom said she wanted me there to make it look like I still owned the company, so I resentfully agreed.

I was in a psychotic mood the morning of the clean-out. We had to move this old green couch and I kept getting cat hair in my mouth while moving the couch. It was making me go insane, have a tantrum, and chew my mom out for making me do this. I feel very sad because that woman thought so much of us and here I am having a breakdown about the company. I was embarrassing myself by losing it when a piece of furniture, covered in cat hair, had a hard time coming out of the house.

I look back on memories of me freaking out about a job or at my friends or around customers, and I feel sorrow. I should have been more level-headed. I was out of my mind with my mental illness and I made that very nice woman have a bad last memory of her parent's house. That breaks me inside...

Mother Knows Best

My grandma had just passed away in Florida. Most of my family had raced to Clearwater to be at her side. Before my grandma passed, she told my mom to buy The Junk Truck from me because of the story of Two Men and a Truck. The company was started by two sons as a side job in college and after graduation, their mother bought the company from them to keep their venture alive. My grandma knew how hard I was suffering from mental illness and addiction and did not want to see The Junk Truck pass away.

Sadly, my grandma wasn't aware of some changes that had taken place in my mother's life. My stepdad was mentally abusive in a silent way. If he got mad, he would walk around the house in silence for at least four straight days. Every door that he opened he would slam behind him in anger. This practice led my mom to isolate herself in her room with her dogs, wine, and a good novel to read. Over time, my mom had morphed into someone different inside; I hardly recognized her by the time that my grandma had passed.

My grandma's last wishes were for my mom to buy The Junk Truck and keep it alive. My grandma wanted me so badly to stop doing junk removal and focus on myself. It was going to be extremely hard to let go of the reins of the junk business to my drunk mom, but I wanted to honor my grandma's wishes. In the aftermath of my grandma's death, my mom and I were feuding with each other because she was making these mysterious choices. My mother started acting very differently. She seemed disinterested in living life anymore. She also treated me like an imposter of junk removal; she seemed to not believe that I could get better. It was very hard to understand the puzzle of my mom's current mode. I kept wondering why my mom was acting like this. My mom was acting removed from life.

For over two weeks, I had been calling my mom and screaming and threatening her life over The Junk Truck. I was in a cannabis psychosis and wasn't ready to let go. I would call my mom and threaten to kill her. Finally, my new girlfriend Ava convinced me to meet my mom at Denny's in Waukesha to hand over the business.

I pulled into the parking lot of Denny's and immediately started crying. I was defeated inside in more ways than I could count. I met my mother inside and we found a seat by the window section. I started crying and asked if me giving up The Junk Truck was honestly the only option. My mom looked at me and started crying. She said this was the only way because of my mental health and addiction. My mom said, "This is what grandma wanted." She promised that she was going to make The Junk Truck just as big as Two Men and a Truck. I cried and agreed it was time to let go of my business. After that exchange, my mom handed me a miniature green urn which held my grandma's ashes. I clenched the urn and let out a wail of sorrow. I was defeated in every way emotionally. I had never felt such pain in my life. Sometimes life turns out the exact opposite you think it will. At the moment, I thought my pain was over; little did I know what was in store the second the business was in my mom's hands...

At Denny's, my mom informed me that she went behind my back and switched the LLC of The Junk Truck into her name. I remember feeling a little violated at the thought of her going behind my back, but I wanted to keep the peace. To be nice, seeing as my mom just gave me a huge portion of her inheritance to buy my junk removal company, I offered to take her and her bastard boyfriend out to dinner to tell her the ins and outs of the junk business. My mom started dating her next manipulator before she even left my abusive stepdad. I remember the day that I met Roller. It was the weirdest circumstances. My mom was finally leaving my abusive stepfather, and me and my girlfriend Ava went to surprise my mom. The second we stepped inside, my mom (sweating profusely) came out of her room which is next to the living area of the lake cottage. Suddenly, this swamp troll (sweating profusely) comes out right behind her.

My first thought was, "Fucking gross! My mom just fucked the Swamp Thing!" I was scared at that moment because I am like, "My mom is going to just jump in bed right with this troll bar-fly. I pulled my mom aside and was like, "You're not going to date that guy right?"

My mom looked at me and said, "Of course not! Me and Roller are just friends!" The next week she moved in with Roller. He had only one hundred dollars to his name when they signed the lease. This was the start of him taking full advantage of my mom financially and isolating her away from all her loved ones.

After I asked to take my mom out to dinner for Junk Truck tips, it was really strange because my mom replied in a way that seemed that she didn't trust me. My mom blurted out that she and Roller had everything covered and that they knew everything. Roller is a fat troll who is a painter, so I seriously doubted that he knew anything about moving junk. I started to feel helpless and questioned why my mom didn't trust me. I just wanted to tell them all the mistakes that I made that I wanted them to avoid. It killed me inside that I then watched my mom make every mistake in the junk removal rulebook because she listened to her bar-fly boyfriend.

The first order of business was to buy two Suburbans that were not rated for hauling the weight junk loads usually were. A few months later, my mom actually bought a real 3500 truck that could pull the dump trailer that they had purchased. My mom then sold one of the Suburbans to a bum from the country that lived in his truck. I watched as this bum took advantage of my mom by never giving her the money for the Suburbans that she shouldn't have bought in the first place. She eventually got the money but it was painful to watch my mom have these drunk losers piddle her inheritance away.

The next mistake was that she bought a dump trailer. I specifically informed her to buy a truck with a bed on it and not a dump trailer. She claimed that Roller had researched all about the dump trailers, but I kept saying that the trailer would take longer to operate the dump in the landfill. Again, time is money, but my mom didn't care. I would question why my mom was acting like this every day.

My girlfriend Ava would always say that my mom had turned into an alcoholic without me noticing. I still couldn't believe it until years later when I was washing the dishes, and her alcoholism hit me like a ton of bricks. It's funny how people you love can disguise their alcoholism, but you won't notice it because of how much you care about them. Anyway, that was only the beginning of her mistakes.

She started booking jobs farther in advance. This was a problem because when a junk customer calls, they need their junk gone usually the same day. What would happen was people would call and my mom would be so sick from drinking that she would put off jobs and people during the week would call a franchised competitor because they could be on top of getting the job done as soon as possible. The next problem was that my mom would roll out of bed after 9. Most junk companies start the engines of their junk trucks by 7:30 AM. By the time we got to a job we were already late and had agitated the customer. It was so painful to watch my business crash and burn that I started by riding through Oconomowoc neighborhoods passing out flyers. I didn't realize that my mom was going to piss on the ashes...

You're Fired!

Real Junk Truck review

Name Withheld ★★★★★ 12/16/2016

What a Great Company! The Junk Truck got rid of years of accumulated crap that was needlessly stored in the crawl space behind our basement. We had to get rid of it before we closed on our house today. I was panicked because I gave the company short notice. But they came through and accommodated my schedule. They truly saved my closing.

This was around the time that I started getting fired by mom. My mom would be too drunk and send me the wrong address, sending me on a wild goose chase. I would bitch about it, and bam! My ass would be fired by my mom. It's weird to be fired multiple times from your own creation. I spent at least two summers on the sidelines because my mom couldn't face up to her shortcomings as the owner of The Junk Truck. My mom was in the throes of her own personal Hell and she started not believing in me. I didn't understand why she would turn her back on me. Every time I would bring up the facts of how she was letting The Junk Truck go to the wayside it would end up in a humongous fight. My mom would end up firing me.

Several times I would call her driving to a job and tell her that I was lost. She would literally just scream at me, "Find it your fucking self!" CLICK!

The bitch would hang up on me while I was driving to her job to make her a few hundred dollars. My brain couldn't compute why she would treat me this way. On top of that, Roller would boss me around like he was some junk journeyman when he didn't even know how to lift items correctly. Roller would say some smartass comment to me and in the middle of the job, I would just get in my car and take off. I didn't fucking care if it was embarrassing for Roller to have to explain that his worker just left halfway through a job. I would go through long periods where I would be "fired" from the Junk Truck, but then my mom would hire me back. It wouldn't be more than two days of work before my mom would pull an alcoholic stunt and I would retaliate and get fired again. It was absolutely embarrassing to experience; my confidence couldn't have been lower. After a while, I didn't even care about the Junk Trucks reputation anymore because I developed a state of mind where I love being in pain. I started to get off on being treated like pig shit because my confidence was nonexistent. My mom claims I was rude, but the real problem lies in the fact that my mom was a bar-fly who was listening to her asshole boyfriend. I went long periods where I wouldn't be a Junk Truck worker and would be forced to sell the things I collected from different jobs just to feed my girlfriend and myself.

My mom liked to pull this stunt where she would only book one job a week that would only last 15 minutes. I would drive my gas hog Bonneville forty miles to someplace like Watertown and then bust out the job in 15 minutes. She would then reward me with a measly twenty dollar bill! She wouldn't even give me gas money! I went from being the owner of The Junk Truck who made over $1,000 a day to a disposable employee who got short-changed with a 20 dollar bill for pity.

I used to cry at night to my girlfriend Ava at the time about how embarrassing this was. I would always spend the 20 on weed because I was ashamed of myself and needed to feel numb. This always left me broke. I couldn't even afford a twinkie from a convenience store without digging in my couch for change. I didn't understand what had changed in my mom's demeanor. I used to ball my eyes out and wish I would die.

The Pool

Real Junk Truck review

Name Withheld ★★★★★ 10/21/2018

I forgot to add in my previous review that they were faced with a tough job, cleaning out the basement of one of my rentals. There was no electricity so they came prepared with lights, headlamps, and respirators.

The only warm memory I have from my mother owning The Junk Truck was a hot tub job in Oconomowoc. My grandpa, my mom, and my grandpa's buddy Matt were hired to remove a hot tub that was next to an inground pool. Junk removal businesses cut the hot tubs up with Sawzalls because of how heavy the tubs are. We then haul them off in four pieces. The pool and hot tub had a black fence surrounding the site, so we pulled the truck and trailer as close as we could to the tub. We started unloading sledgehammers and the saw. My grandpa took a pair of bolt cutters and without asking, cut the thick cord of the hot tub. BOOM! Sparks go flying and so does my grandpa. He is so lucky that the bolt cutters had rubber handles! We never found out, but I guarantee we blew a circuit in the house. In my head, I was mad because when I owned the business, I always asked if the tubs were disconnected.

We all were kind of shaken by the mishap, but we started to get prepared to saw the tub into four pieces. We all kind of brainstormed how to get the tub over the fence once it was cut into four manageable pieces. Some hot tubs have a ridiculous amount of insulation lining the hoses that are connected to the jets; this happened to be a motherfucker of a tub. We all sat there while my grandpa used the Sawzall and cut into the hot tub. It got to the point where using a sledgehammer might break some of the cuts loose to divide the tub. Matt took a couple of whacks and it wasn't budging. It was at that moment that we noticed there were bees living in the bottom of the tub. They started buzzing around us in little waves at first. We were all concerned about the bee problem, but the pests didn't seem pissed off. Enter my presence! Leave it to me to completely piss off the bees!

I suddenly grabbed the sledge for some reason and started beating the tub like it owed me money. Everyone started screaming to stop, but I wanted to prove that I still got it in the junk business. The bees started swarming causing everyone to run for their lives. I jumped the fence, Matt took off toward the other side of the fence, and my grandpa took off running but ran right into the deep end of the pool. When my grandpa ran and fell in the pool, it literally looked like a televangelist trying to imitate Jesus walking on water. The whole Junk Truck team stopped in place and started hysterically laughing. My grandpa swam over like a golden retriever to the pool steps and climbed out with his clothes waterlogged. After I stopped laughing, I looked and said, "Let me give you a ride home for fresh clothes."

We got in my silver Pontiac Bonneville and I drove him to his house for a change of garments. On the way, my grandpa said, "I told you one of us would end up in that pool!"

The Fish Tank

Most of the time, Roller and I would never get along. I wanted to just scream when he took over at the Junk Truck because he would like to refuse certain jobs. He was alienating potential lifelong clients. On one job in particular, I agreed to not do a certain task for the junk job, but I would usually give it the college try.

I drove my Pontiac Bonneville the 40 miles to Oconomowoc from my house in Milwaukee. I met them at the old Oconomowoc Middle School for a job in the neighborhood of older houses. We pulled up to a house that was forest green and looked dilapidated.

It is always a good sign when the customer meets with you shirtless. This guy with no fucking shirt showed up with his son who looked like he listens to Adema. They showed Roller and me all this junk outside. The house looked like the Hollywood set of Sanford and Son.

We told them, "We can definitely tackle this for you."

They then took us upstairs to their house. The stairs were falling apart. One step with heavy junk and we might fall to the basement. They showed us the biggest glass fish tank I have ever seen with mold growing inside. The guy said, "Yeah, this is going to go also."

Roller and I both looked at each other and he said, "We can't take that fish tank down those stairs. They are rotting and falling apart. We could be cut in half."

The guy was pissed and started arguing, "Me and my son took the tank upstairs 10 years ago! It can be done!"

"That is my point! That was 10 years ago! In that time, the stairs have deteriorated." The father and son were mad, so we loaded everything else up in the trailer. It was the one time I agreed with not taking an item for fear of our safety, but otherwise, Roller was plain embarrassing as a Junk Truck representative.

Roller would drink a ton of coffee on the way to the job and, like clockwork, the second phrase out his mouth after "Hi" was, "I'm sorry! Can I use your bathroom?" What a good first impression that was for my past customers. A fat troll using their sacred bathroom. Roller was like Bulk and Skull from the Power Rangers. He was an embarrassment...

Marilyn Designs

Real Junk Truck review

Name Withheld ★★★★★ 2/9/2017

These guys are great. Young, ambitious, and striving to do an excellent job. I would hire them again.

Once my mom owned The Junk Truck, she loved to do this thing where she would force me to still pretend I owned The Junk Truck. On jobs where clients would ask for me specifically, my mom would have me stop by and act like I wasn't an insane maniac. I would get asked for by name by a lot of real estate agents, so I would have to go wave like I'm Colonel Sanders. "Here is your chicken corpse Travis!" All my mom would have to do is resurrect me from my THC Tomb. I would stop by and say hey! It killed me emotionally inside a lot because I could not move on from the failure of my business. I was being treated differently by all my friends now. My world was caving in on me.

I got booked for my usual Junk Truck acting gig. I was to pretend that I was still the owner in front of this realtor that was ranting and raving about me. When we rolled up to the property, the realtor (who hired us) was waiting outside for us. The realtor made me come out of the truck. The realtor said, "Travis! You're real! You're really at a job!"

I got flustered and manic inside as I swallowed a lump in my throat. I awkwardly said, "Of course I'm real! I am just doing other jobs." The realtor looked puzzled but was just happy to know that I was alive. It felt like every minute I had to be reminded of my biggest failure. I was quickly relieved though when we started to observe the junk job scenario. The job was a hoarding situation for a mother and daughter duo. We needed to get to work right away. We had trouble backing up our two trucks and trailers in the tight spaces of the condo complex.

There were four of us doing the junk job. Roller, Mom, Ava, and me. The two women of the house were having anxiety attacks about stuff that was going to be chucked. These are hoarders who will drag their feet every step of the way making it impossible for the new homeowners to take over. The condo was a 3-bedroom 2-bath unit with a basement and garage. Each room was a disaster with junk strewn everywhere. Before we went in, the realtor warned us that the duo hadn't boxed or packed anything for us to remove. She also warned us that there was a ton of stuff that had to go.

They planned to close the next day, but the house looked like they woke up and said, "Maybe we should call some movers!" The house was bulging with junk and it looked like they hadn't packed one box for the big move. I was laughing inside because I knew it wouldn't be possible to move all the junk they have in a day. With one junk removal truck, you can only haul out 1-3 loads before the dump closes for the day. They should have called weeks ago! We started to load up the junk into the trailers. The mother and daughter hoarding team started to have tantrums about stuff they had to part with. The mother owned a shop downtown that had an apartment above the storefront. They were downsizing into that apartment. Needless to say, they needed to junk a lot of their possessions to fit in their new dwelling. They would freak out about parting with half-used potting soil. Usually, I am in good spirits with hoarders, but I was in my own personal Hell with having to experience my feelings. I was just snapping inside. Marilyn [the mother] sat at her kitchen table and cried about us moving her stuff to the trailer. We were moving at a fast pace to try to get done before the closing, but Marilyn left for the closing while the job wasn't even halfway done. The realtor came back from the closing and told us some gossip. She told us that the new homeowners were super pissed off at Marilyn because of her possessions not being out of the house.

Marilyn and her daughter had really big decisions with parting on stuff that I still think about today. They were losing their world around them. Sometimes people will put off something that they know is hard to face. The realtor kept telling Marilyn to let us take the stuff until it was just about all cleared out. The energy was scattered and frantic, but eventually, Marilyn dealt with her new life change. In more ways than one, I was dealing with scattered and frantic energy because of a new life change myself.

The Fallen Empire

Real Junk Truck review

Name Withheld ★★★★★ 10/30/2017

Great service! I've used them
before and will use them again.

By this point, we were beating a dead
horse by keeping The Junk Truck open. My mother
and I had a very strained relationship, we were
both addicted to chemicals, and my mom literally
was miserable running the business. I would hear
from clients how different the phone calls were
when clients would book jobs. My mom had a big
habit of not calling people back, so we lost a lot of
my client list. I wanted to convince my mom to
close the business down. We had a job to do out in
Dodge County. I had to ride with Roller. The whole
way to the job we both bitched about how my mom
didn't care about running the business correctly.
We both knew my mom wasn't cut out to be a junk
woman because she wouldn't start a job until
around 10 AM, would do crappy work for
customers, and she had become bitter.

When I got back, I confronted my mom
about putting the nail in the coffin on The Junk
Truck. My mom started out saying, "I promised
Grandma that I would make this like Two Men And
A Truck."

This time I didn't yell at her. I basically let my mom down easy and made what my past therapists have called a "criticism sandwich". You start out with saying something positive for the bread, the middle is the criticism, and the bottom bun is another form of positivity. I could tell my mom wanted to honor our fallen grandmother, but I kept assuring her that grandma wouldn't want us to be living this way. My mom and I were both addicts and extremely unhappy with our current lives. My mom finally broke down and agreed to give it up. I made my mom promise this would be the last time we would do junk removal. I made her promise The Junk Truck would be good and dead. The last nail would strike the coffin of my creation. I said, "I don't want The Junk Truck to come back from the dead."

She agreed. My mom said, "We are done doing junk removal!" For a moment life seemed to be working out the way it should. I felt like I could finally breathe after being taken on that hell ride.

D.J.W. Junk Removal

Real Junk Truck review

Name Withheld ★ 10/30/2018

I booked an appointment, which they canceled the day before claiming their trailer's axle broke. The job was rescheduled for the following week. They never showed up, and when I called to find out what was going on, I got voicemail. They never returned my call.

Two days after the final Junk Truck Job, my mom sold the dump trailer to her skeevy boyfriend, Roller. I asked my mom, "What is Roller going to do with the trailer?" My mom seemed excited and said, "Roller is starting his own junk removal business!" My mom also said, "The new company is called DJW because we are only going to service Dodge, Jefferson, and Waukesha Counties! We aren't going to even do jobs in Milwaukee!" I was fucking stunned and so fucking angry. Basically, Roller made us close down the business so he could buy that trailer cheap from my mom. He really fucking took advantage of my mom in this situation. I started fucking screaming about how she had lied to me and how much of a piece of shit Roller was. I could not fucking believe it.

My mom came dancing in the room singing, "I just made 20 dollars!"

I asked, "How?"

My mom eagerly told me, "Roller gives me 20 bucks every time I bring in a lead!"

My mom was cherry-picking my client list for her scumbag boyfriend! I called my Aunt Stacey and started to threaten my mom and Roller's lives. It took me 8 years to build up a huge client list of happy customers and now Ernest P. Worrell was going to destroy my reputation. When this kind of shit happens, it is a silent scream. You want to scream, but who will hear you? I just wanted to jump out of my flesh with my skeleton. Another problem was that most of my family didn't see what my mom was doing. My mom told my aunt that she would stop, but I'm pretty sure she never did.

I was such an addict that I needed money so badly that I asked if I could work for DJW Junk Removal. Roller and my mom literally couldn't believe it! Roller asked my mom, "Would Travis really do that? Work for me?" He couldn't even believe I would stoop so low down to his level.

Sometimes I like to do the most demeaning things because I hate myself so much. I was so beaten down by life! I did a few jobs for them until Roller finally realized he wasn't cut out for junk removal. We would be on the way to a job and he would finish fast. He would have another job to do but he would always say I will just get them done another day! I was driving from Milwaukee 40 miles to do the jobs that my mom had set up for us and he wanted to just do one small job. I couldn't fucking live off of one little job a week whenever Roller felt like it. Doing a junk job was so far and few between, that I just quit. The other part of the scenario was that D.J.W. Junk Removal wasn't a real business. When Roller would finish a job he would ask for the check to be made out to him personally instead of an established business identity.

I always think about how bad the ending of the Junk Truck was, but it had a lot to do with my mother's alcoholism and my mental illness and addiction. We both ran the company into the ground.

Epilogue

It has been over half a decade since my incarnation of The Junk Truck was rolling down the road. Through all the heartache and sorrow, I have found myself at a level place in life. In the years since the trailer got raided, I have found peace in performing improv comedy, scare acting at haunted attractions, and, of course, writing. These creative outlets helped me forge a new identity for myself at a time when I didn't want to be me. My mental illness has reared its head in a few spots since the company has closed, but I feel like I am in a very stable place in my life for once. I have made big changes in my life since the events of yesteryear. Currently, I just got back from Muncie, Indiana. My girl and I did the Garfield Trail. As a lifelong Garfield Fanatic, it has been a dream of mine to see the Garfield Mecca that is Muncie and Grant County. There are over 30 Garfield statues to see around the East-Central Indiana area. While in Muncie, I got engaged to my best friend. These are pretty big moves for someone who never took a vacation or believed there was a future that lay ahead for him. Coming back from Muncie, I was faced with my biggest forms of adversity. My mother. I decided to not have a relationship with my mother. I went for a walk at nature hill in Oconomowoc, and I called my fiance to tell her about my decision.

My fiance said, "I am really happy that you are making that decision to not let your alcoholic mother affect you. I probably shouldn't tell you this but when we first started dating your mother said some horrible things about you. I was talking about the life I wanted to have with you and your mom said, 'Honey! There is no life with Travis! He will always be too sick.'"

When Emma said that to me, it was like I didn't want to be anywhere. I wanted to run out of the woods of Nature Hill and go kill myself. I always questioned why my mother didn't believe in me after The Junk Truck ended, but now I had proof that she didn't. It took a lot of courage to face that thought. It took even more courage to not kill myself. I suffered from a severe mental illness most of my life, but that doesn't define me. Do I not deserve happiness? The answer is, "yes."

It has taken a lot of work to rebuild the life that I destroyed. It has taken doctors, therapy, and the right medication to become a stable person that can fit into society. I have to work every single day towards staying in a good place. I see my doctor every two months to make sure that I am not slipping with my type one bipolar disorder. I talk every single week to a therapist that helps me decipher what happened to me in my life. In the past, I have been involved in mental illness support groups. A good mixture of these activities and it is possible to stay in reality.

As for my mother, I had to be able to let her go. I didn't realize she was a raging alcoholic when I gave her my business. Alcoholism reveals itself very slowly in the eyes of a loved one. I would always ask my ex Ava, "Why is my mom acting like this? Why would she do this to me?" The answer came to me one day when I was washing the dishes. The sun was beaming through the blinds in front of the sink, I was washing a dish, and it hit me like a ton of bricks. I realized my mother was an alcoholic. I had been so blind because she was my mother, but it was true. My mom was checked out in life; that kills me, but I can't let her hold me down any longer. It is very hard to watch loved ones suffer, but they need to want help. I don't even know if Dr. Phil could solve the strain of my mother and I's relationship. She is in denial about what she put me through. It would be very hard to forgive her after the wreckage of our past.

Life is very strange. Maybe one day we will reconnect somewhere down the road...

The End

Acknowledgments

This book would not exist without Emma Lenar. Thank you for the support and encouragement to write this book. I love you deeply. Thank you, Emma, for standing by me when no one else would. A big thank you to Lucas Lenar and the entire Lenar Family. Next, I would like to thank the amazing author Laura Lemke for always giving me advice on my writing. Laura's work can be seen at https://lllemkewrites.wordpress.com/

I would like to thank my Grandpa Geier for always believing in me with my improv, writing, and life. I love you, Grandpa! Next, I would like to thank my Grandma Niece (RIP). I miss you every day. I wish you here to read this book and to know that I am okay. I want to send a big thank you to my Aunt Stacey and Uncle Dave. You guys are my heroes! A big shout out to my favorite Yellow Lab Summer. Thank you to all the retired greyhounds I have adopted. I love you Willow Run Chalk, Rum Toby Tipper, N.B.'s Sugar Cat, and Ponda's Fiction!

I would like to personally thank the Waukesha County Technical College Learning Center, specifically Jon, Sandy, Bette, and Maureen. Thank you for giving me the dignity of communication through writing.

Thank you to Pete Schlosser for all your guidance and mentorship. A big thank you to Trevor Adonis (RIP) for the advice. I would like to thank Lisa Young for being the book's first fan. A big thank you to the following Wisconsin businesses: Burkhambuilt.com, Radtkeappliance.com, Waterpop.art, Lombardolawoffice.com, Mudtechworks.com, brandonevans.art, Dog in Suds Grooming Salon, Your Auto Repair (West Allis), The Pass It On Club, Fox Music Company, and Breakshots Huba Huba Bar and Grill.

Lastly, I would like to thank every customer and employee that ever let me into their lives. Thank you for your years of support at The Junk Truck.

About the Author

Travis Geier was born in Milwaukee but raised in Ixonia, Wisconsin. Travis is best known for his role in Wisconsin junk removal. He owned The Junk Truck, worked for Junk King, and finished his career with College Hunks Hauling Junk. He ran The Junk Truck for close to 10 years before deep diving into creative ventures. In entertainment, Travis has acted in some of the scariest haunted attractions in the Midwest. He also has played countless long-form improv comedy shows. He maintained a blog at travisvulture.com detailing his struggles with mental illness. Travis currently resides in Milwaukee, Wisconsin with his retired greyhound, Fiction.